BEYOND CHOICE

BEYOND CHOICE

The Abortion Story No One is Telling

DON BAKER

MULTNOMAH · PRESS

Portland, Oregon 97266

The names of the people and places appearing in this book have been changed to maintain the anonymity of the persons involved.

Cover design by Paul Lewis

Cover photo by Russ Keller
Edited by Larry R. Libby

BEYOND CHOICE
© 1985 by Don Baker
Published by Multnomah Press
Portland, Oregon 97266

Printed in the United States of America

Contents

Preface

Since the Roe V. Wade Supreme Court decision in 1973, it is estimated that there have been somewhere between ten and fifteen million abortions in the United States. One in three pregnancies ends in abortion.

Pro-abortionists have argued in favor of abortion as a matter of freedom of choice. "A woman should have the right to make decisions that pertain to her own body," they say.

Pro-lifers have argued against abortion from the same position. "An unborn child should not be deprived of his freedom. He should be accorded the same rights that are given to the woman who bears him."

Freedom of choice does not mean freedom from consequence. Every choice has its own consequence. Some consequences are good . . . some are bad. Some are temporary . . . some linger . . . some may never be changed.

Beyond Choice is the story of a woman who chose to terminate three pregnancies by abortion. The story is based on truth. Identities and locations have been altered to disguise true names and places.

The book takes its readers behind the scenes to explore an unwed mother's childhood and sexual encounters.

It takes the reader into three abortion clinics to observe the counseling procedures and the actual surgical process.

It takes the reader into a woman's mind and heart to see and feel the struggles that take place within.

It takes the reader into her marriage to better understand

Beyond Choice

some of the possible complications of a freedom that may just have a hook in it.

Beyond Choice is just one woman's story . . . but it may be the story of millions who have never had the courage or the opportunity to tell it all.

Don Baker

CHAPTER ONE

Debbie watched the light snowflakes drift by her window as she lay fully clothed on a twin-sized bed in the silence of her lonely room. She stared blankly at the collection of rock stars that lined her soft pink walls. She scanned the music and scholastic awards she had won in her nearly two and one-half years at Jefferson High School. Her eyes lingered on the collection of foreign dolls perched on top of her bookcase and finally stopped to stare at a little brown teddy bear, its eyes pulled out and its fur long since rubbed bare, propped limply on a little maple rocking chair in the corner.

Her radio was silent . . . nothing it could say held any meaning. Her telephone was still . . . its expectant ring throttled by an angry father who had ripped its cord from the wall.

Debbie was a prisoner . . . a prisoner in her own home . . . her own bedroom . . . waiting for the moment when her crime would feel the full weight of its sentence.

Her crime . . . a few moments of sensual pleasure. Her punishment . . . a pregnancy that must now be terminated by abortion.

For more than a week Debbie had been confined to her room. All her meals had been delivered at the door. The only conversation was an occasional clipped, "Here's your food," as her mother would hand her a tray, promptly retreat, and close the door behind her. Debbie was allowed out to go to the bathroom—and that was all.

There had been one exception. On Christmas Day she had been permitted to gather around the tree with her family for a very somber celebration.

For ten days Debbie talked to a stuffed toy that lay unresisting on her arm.

For ten days Debbie wished for a miracle that didn't happen.

For ten days Debbie relived one night she wanted to erase forever.

For ten days Debbie cursed and Debbie cried and Debbie prayed to a God she really didn't know.

For ten days Debbie waited for the nightmare to end only to realize that this was no dream. This was agonizingly real and it would only end when her parents had their demands fully met.

"It's time to go, Deborah." Her mother's voice was cold—flat. She flung open the door and threw Debbie's heavy jacket on the bed. With a sigh, Debbie straightened her clothes, slipped her arms into the bulky sleeves, and slowly followed her parents out the front door to the car.

All three were silent as they drove down the long, winding hill to the suburban mall that housed the Columbia River Medical Clinic. The time for reasoning, the time for argument, the time for any appeal was long since past.

All three, father, mother, and sixteen-year-old daughter had exhausted all the energy and emotion they could afford. The only thing left was to do what had to be done . . . as quickly and as quietly as possible.

The waiting room was nearly full when they arrived. Most of the women were young . . . in their late teens. They were accompanied by what appeared to be very troubled and very silent boyfriends.

Debbie's mother and father were the only parents present. There were no children.

They were greeted by a friendly receptionist who checked Debbie's name off the appointment sheet and asked, "Do you have the money?" Debbie moved back from the desk and looked at her father.

"How much is it?" he asked, as he pulled his checkbook

from his inside coat pocket.

"Two hundred and twenty-five dollars."

"Two hundred and twenty-five dollars for fifteen minutes with a doctor?" he exploded.

"Yes, sir, two hundred and twenty-five dollars, and it may take longer. Debbie will be here for about three hours. And sir," she added apologetically, "that will have to be cash. I'm sorry— but we don't accept personal checks."

"Will you take a credit card?"

"I'm sorry, sir, but we can't accept credit cards either. You will notice it says here on this information form that 'Our fee is two hundred and twenty-five dollars. We will accept the payment in cash, money order, or a cashier's check. We do not accept personal checks. This is the total fee and includes a Rhogram injection if the patient is Rh negative.' "

"I don't have that much cash with me. You'll have to wait until I go to the bank—or do we have to make another appointment?"

"It will be a week before Dr. Jeffers will be back in Hood River again, sir. I'd suggest that we keep this appointment. Debbie has a number of forms to fill out before she meets with the counselor, and if necessary, we'd be happy to wait until your return."

Debbie could feel every eye in the room fixed on her during this verbal exchange, and was relieved to take the clipboard with the accompanying medical forms to one of the brightly colored vinyl chairs in a distant corner.

She leafed through four sheets of paper. One was a medical history form. The next was more personal and stated that it was confidential and to be used for statistical purposes only. The third was a consent form, and the last was for the counselor and the doctor to sign.

Debbie wished she could avoid some of the questions. She didn't mind filling in the time of arrival or her name, address, and phone number, but when she was asked for her marital status, it was difficult to acknowledge that she was unmarried.

That certainly wasn't the way she wanted it. She and Tim had talked about marriage since the time of their first date. Neither could wait to get away from home. Debbie had never dreamed that there was another whose father and mother were as difficult to live with as hers. She had been sure that her life was the world's most miserable and her family was the community's most difficult . . . until she met Tim.

He looked just like Bjorn Borg, she thought as she watched him put away his notebook in the orange locker just across the hall from hers.

"Isn't he cute?" she said to Karen. "What's his name?"

"Don't you know who that is, Deb? That's Tim Beezley. He's Jefferson's hopes for all sorts of track records this year. Do you want to meet him?"

"Sure, why not."

It didn't take long after that first introduction for Tim and Debbie to realize just how much they were meant for each other. Every afternoon Debbie and Karen would hurry out to the field to sit in the bleachers and watch Tim work through his rigorous routine. When he was finished, she'd rush over to him and together they'd walk back to the gym.

Every school day ended with at least fifteen minutes at Bennett's lingering over a Coke and talking about how very much they had in common.

Debbie wanted to be a nurse . . . Tim a motorcycle mechanic. "Not the most ambitious goal in the world," he would say, "but I love cycles. I just can't get enough of them. Build them, ride them, fix them. Someday I want to design them. I have a dream for a cycle that's never been built."

Debbie would listen to Tim dream, then share her own. It was so much fun to dream for a change. It was so much fun to talk, to listen, to be heard, and to be loved. It was so different from the nightmare she had been forced to endure for as long as she could remember.

She couldn't recall a time when anyone in her home seemed to be genuinely interested in her. She was the first of four children to be born in just five and a half years. Her mother was always too busy with babies to give time to Debbie.

"I'm too busy now, we'll talk about it later," was a phrase she had come to expect whenever she asked anything of her mother. Whenever she made noise, she was told to be quiet. Whenever she wanted to play, she was forced to work. Whenever she wanted to go outside, she was told to stay in. Whenever she wanted to stay in, she was forced to go out. She never knew where she belonged or why.

On her tenth birthday, Debbie was given a surprise party. Her parents' tenth anniversary celebration was just a few weeks before her birthday party. Just before going to bed that night, she said to her mother, "I was born at almost the same time you and daddy were married, wasn't I?" It was an innocent question . . . it wasn't meant as an accusation . . . in fact, to Debbie it was a happy thought that she and her parents had something so important in common.

"Shut up and go to bed," she was told. "That's none of your business! I don't want you to ever talk about that again."

She lay softly sobbing for a long time that night wondering what she had said or done that could have caused such anger to spoil what had been one of the few beautiful days in her lifetime.

Church consisted of confession, communion, and contra-fraternity, and she didn't understand the meaning of any of them. The services were in Latin and the ritual was as foreign as the language.

She would spend her time counting candles or looking at the carved forms of patron saints or trying to understand the actions of a white-robed man who could never remember her name.

Debbie didn't like church at all. The only time it was ever referred to in her home was when her parents would tell her she couldn't do something, because her church didn't approve.

Debbie's dad came home from work drunk almost every night. She got so she would start watching the clock late in the afternoon and grow increasingly nervous as the time for his arrival neared. After 5:30, she always knew what to expect. There would be an empty place at the table, an angry mother, and four silent children. Dad would come in later, curse his wife, scatter the children, and make life miserable until bedtime.

Tim seemed to be the perfect solution to all her problems, and as Tim described his home life, she was convinced that he needed her as much as she needed him.

CHAPTER TWO

What was the day of your last normal period? Debbie studied the question carefully. She knew she had missed at least two periods, but then she wasn't always regular with her menstrual cycle. She had been asked this on the day of her pregnancy test and she had guessed then that it had been at least two months. For a number of weeks she had been feeling tired and occasionally dizzy. Her mornings had been the most difficult time, and her clothes had begun to feel more snug than usual.

She finally decided that she could be at least twelve weeks pregnant and filled in the form accordingly.

She stated that her pregnancy had been confirmed at the Planned Parenthood Center, that this was her first, that she had never had a Caesarean section, and that she did not have an IUD (loop, shield, or coil) in her uterus.

No, she did not have any recent medical problems. No, she was not under treatment for any illness. No, she was not sensitive to any drugs—at least she didn't think so. She showed the form to her mother, who didn't know of any either.

No, she was not taking any drugs routinely, and no, she had never bled heavily after an operation or childbirth.

Debbie agreed that the above information was correct to the best of her knowledge, and then signed her name.

As she turned to the next page, she paused and looked around the brightly decorated area and noticed that two of the waiting room chairs were empty. She had not been aware of any movement or of anyone's name being called.

She was relieved to notice that the next page was not to be signed. It simply stated, "This additional information will be used for statistical purposes only. Your name will not be connected with this information."

She filled in the routine questions that asked for the name of her city, county, and state. She had completed her second year in high school, was not employed, was sixteen years of age, unmarried, white, and Catholic.

Do you generally practice contraception?

This question both amused and angered her. If I generally practiced contraception, I sure wouldn't be here, she thought. But then, I don't generally have intercourse.

Contraceptive devices had been foreign to Debbie until recently. Planned Parenthood had just demonstrated the different forms of contraception on two nearly life-sized plastic models. They had described the various birth control methods and shown how and where they were to be used.

"Sex is a natural thing that happens between people," they had explained. "There is nothing wrong with sex; there's no reason for you to feel guilty about having sex. The only thing wrong with sex is that you may become pregnant. These pills and devices are designed to keep that from happening. Even if you should become pregnant, there is a provision for that, also. Planned Parenthood is established to assist you in securing an abortion which is a simple, painless procedure designed to remove the foreign matter from your body and end your pregnancy. No one needs to know anything about it; it will have no damaging effects on your body, and you'll still be able to get pregnant when you want to. There's no need for your parents to hassle you, and in most cases, they'll not even need to know."

Debbie remembered that presentation and recalled that they had actually made sex sound like a lot of fun. That was so different from the few remarks her parents had made to her.

Did your pregnancy follow from temporarily omitting the method of contraception?

She was confused as to how this was to be answered. She

didn't have a method of contraception, so she couldn't say that she had temporarily omitted its use. She left the answer blank.

As she moved to make herself more comfortable in the chair, she glanced quickly at her mother to be sure she was still reading a magazine. Some of these questions were far too personal for even her mother's eyes.

What method was used? (Circle one)

Pill, diaphragm, foam/jelly, condom, foam/condom, rhythm, withdrawal, other, specify _____.

This question really wasn't hard to answer, but it was extremely difficult to write on a piece of paper. With reluctance, she drew a circle around the word *withdrawal* and then added "But not in time."

What were your reason(s) for not using contraception?

Lack of knowledge
Lack of availability
Lack of confidentiality
Lack of money
Refused by physician
Religious reasons
Other _____
Not applicable
Unknown

There was only one answer that Debbie could check . . . a contraceptive device was not available. She and Tim had never thought they would have to use one. Their first and only sexual encounter was totally unplanned, and by her, at least, totally unexpected.

It had happened after an exciting football game. They had planned to celebrate the victory at Bennett's but found themselves heading away from the crowd . . . away from the town.

Tim pulled Debbie's 1971 Chevy Malibu into a scenic view area that overlooked the Columbia. The mighty river looked calm and serene that night, shimmering in the light of a nearly full moon. The September evening was balmy, with a slight breeze. It was very quiet.

They sat together, enjoying the silence for awhile, and then began to relive what for both of them had been a terribly bad day.

"I wish I didn't have to go back home tonight," said Tim. "I'm not sure how much longer I can stand my folks. I can never please them. You know, Deb, I think if I made straight A's in all of my classes, won three Olympic Gold Medals in Track, and became a millionaire in business, they'd still find something to complain about."

"I'm sorry," whispered Debbie as she moved closer to Tim and took his hand in hers.

"Maybe if we move away from our parents . . . neither of us is happy at home. I can't talk to anyone but you. Nobody else listens to me, nobody else hears me . . . only you, Debbie. Why don't we drop out of school and get married? I probably won't get rich fixing bikes for a long time but we could at least get us a little mobile home. I think I can support you. I know at least I can love you and that's something neither of us is getting now."

Debbie loved the words she was hearing. She had never heard words like this before. She had never felt such intensity, such warmth, such fullness. She was so full, she wanted to cry . . . so happy, she wanted to laugh.

She let Tim put his arm around her and pull her close. She felt an urgency in her mind and in her body that she had never sensed before. When Tim suggested they climb into the back seat, she didn't hesitate.

It hurt. It hurt a lot . . . and she bled. This frightened her and embarrassed them both. There had been no bright flashes of light, no feelings of ecstasy, no orgasm. In fact, her first sexual encounter had been disappointing and uncomfortable and messy. But it felt so good to be close, to be hugged, to be warm. She had wished it could last forever.

Tim cried. His tears startled Debbie until she heard him say, "Nothing can come between us now, Debbie. I'm going to marry you. I have finally found someone who really loves me and someone I really love."

They drove home in silent fulfillment, holding tightly to each other's hands, savoring the moment and dreaming of a lifetime.

Four weeks later Debbie began to suspect that she was pregnant.

CHAPTER THREE

What are your reasons for terminating this pregnancy?

Finances
Age
Family size
Health
Partner has left
Partner relationship in doubt
Future plans
Parental pressure
Partner pressure
Don't wish to parent at this time
Other

There was no hesitancy whatever in Debbie's answer to this question. Abortion had not been her idea. It certainly wasn't Tim's idea. She wanted to keep this baby. She wanted to get married.

She marked a wide X alongside *Parental pressure* and then drew circles around those two words. Suddenly she felt intense hatred toward the woman seated beside her, toward her father, and even toward her high school principal.

Debbie had hoped to keep her secret as long as possible. As soon as symptoms of pregnancy began to occur, she went to the

Planned Parenthood Center for a pregnancy test.

"Did you bring a urine sample?" she was asked. "Yes," she answered.

"Is it the first A.M. sample?"

"Yes."

The lady who took the sample was friendly and concerned. She told Debbie to call back after 3:30 in the afternoon.

Debbie made the call from the bedroom phone. As she was talking, her father walked by her open door. "Hi, Deb," he called, "I didn't know you were home."

"Hi, Dad, yeah, I'm home." She tried hard to keep the fear as well as the tears out of her voice. She had just heard the news that the test was positive. She was pregnant. "Come in tomorrow and we'll talk about it," the voice on the phone was telling her.

As soon as she could hang up the phone, Debbie called Tim. "The test was positive, Tim. I'm pregnant." She began to cry.

"Oh God . . . really? There's no mistake? Debbie, you *can't* be pregnant. We only made love one time. You just can't be pregnant!"

"I'm sorry, Tim. I really didn't do this on purpose. I didn't mean for this to happen. I'm sorry. What are we going to do?"

"We'll get married, Deb," Tim said without hesitating. "That's our baby and this is one way we can get away from our homes and start one of our own. I'll go to work and you'll finish school. I don't know what I'll do without any education, but I'll go to work and I'll support you and I'll support our baby. Don't worry, Deb, it's going to be all right . . . you'll see."

Tim and Debbie began to dream again. They quickly forgot their problem and began thinking of baby names and of mobile homes and of jobs and of a wedding. They decided to keep the secret to themselves. No one was to know . . . no one.

Two weeks later, Debbie was called out of class to report to the office of the principal. She walked slowly through the long third story hallway, down two flights of stairs, past dozens of orange lockers, including her own and Tim's, to the door marked "Office."

She hesitated for a long time before going in. Mrs. Swenson seemed unusually curt this morning and said nothing more than, "Mr. Timms is waiting for you."

This was not her first trip to this office. Mr. Timms was not only Debbie's principal, but also her next-door neighbor and a long-time friend of the family's. She had been here often . . . but always on friendly business. She loved the way he had furnished this room . . . an old oak roll-top desk, a long conference table with straight-back chairs, and walls covered with knickknacks, and pictures and mementos from graduating classes . . . and she loved Mr. Timms.

There was no friendliness this time. Mr. Timms's manner was detached and cold. His statement was brief and blunt. "Debbie, I hear you're pregnant."

Debbie dissolved in tears. She reached out to touch her friend. She hoped that there might be the same welcome hug she had felt so many times. Mr. Timms just stood there, arms to his side, a stern look on his face.

"How far along are you?" he asked.

"I don't know," sobbed Debbie. "I just found out for sure the other day . . . Maybe six weeks or it may even be more."

"Who's the boy?" he demanded.

Debbie was silent.

"Is it Tim Beezley?"

Without thinking, Debbie answered, "Yes."

"Your folks will have to know immediately." Mr. Timms reached for his phone.

Debbie sat down, buried her head in her hands, and sobbed. There was no resistance left in her. She knew that any argument was useless at this point. She listened to the urgency in Mr. Timms's voice as he explained to her parents that he must see them immediately.

The Porters arrived within minutes. They listened with unbelief as they were told that Debbie Porter . . . their daughter . . . was pregnant.

They said only three things that Debbie could remember . . . three things, in fact, that she would never forget . . .

"Who did this?"

Mr. Timms answered their question.

"Why have you done this to us?" To this question, there was no answer.

"You're going to have an abortion."

"I am not," Debbie answered loudly and quickly. "I am going to have my baby and I am going to keep my baby. Tim and I are going to be married and there's nothing you can do about it. I love Tim and I love my baby."

"How can you love a blob?" her mother shouted. "All it is is just a blob of jelly. You're going to have an abortion. I won't let a blob of jelly ruin your whole life and force you into a marriage that's not good for you."

"If it's so bad, why didn't you abort me?" screamed Debbie. "You were pregnant when you got married."

"It wasn't legal then, or I would have," screamed her mother in response.

Something in Debbie died in that moment. She turned white . . . her tears stopped flowing . . . her words choked back down into her throat . . . her body went limp. Her worst fears were realized. There was nothing more to say. Her mother had just said it all. She had just confirmed all that Debbie had feared and felt. She was not wanted and never had been.

The battle was over. The parents had won. Debbie went home to the seclusion of her room, to wait.

She called Tim that night. As she told him all that had happened, he began to cry.

"I've got to see you, Debbie."

"You can't."

"I've got to call you."

"You can't."

"We've got to get away."

"We can't, Tim. There's nothing we can do." Debbie's father threw her bedroom door open, grabbed the phone from her hand, and yanked its cord from the wall.

"If I ever get my hands on that kid, I'll kill him," he shouted, "and if you ever talk to him again, I think I'll kill you."

The forms in her hands were shaking and wet with tears as Debbie looked up to see her father counting out two hundred and twenty-five dollars and reluctantly handing the bills to the receptionist.

Debbie continued to read through the forms. The third page was a consent form and required her signature before the abortion could be administered. She read it carefully.

> I. I,_____, do hereby request and give my authorization and consent to abortion, to be performed on me by Dr. Arnold Jeffers, M.D., of the

Columbia River Medical Clinic. I further certify that an explanation of the abortion procedure was discussed, along with the accompanying risks and alternatives.

II. I also consent that during, preceding, and following the operation, said doctor may perform any other procedure he deems necessary or desirable in order to perform the abortion or to treat any unhealthy condition that may be encountered during or because of the abortion.

III. I further realize that an abortion by modern methods requires the cooperation of numerous technicians and other personnel and I give my further consent to ministrations and medical procedures on my body, by all such qualified medical personnel working under the supervision of said doctor, before, during and after the operation to be performed.

IV. I consent to the administration of anesthetic to be administered by or under the direction of said doctor and to the use of such anesthetics as may be deemed advisable in my case.

V. I know that the practice of medicine and surgery is not an exact science and that reputable practitioners cannot properly guarantee results. I acknowledge that no guarantee or assurances have been made by anyone regarding the operation which I have requested and authorized. I understand that certain unfavorable results may follow from the operation, including, but not limited to, pain and suffering, bleeding, sterility and emotional upset.

Debbie paused for a long time after reading this paragraph. She had never read a legal form in her life. Many of the words were foreign. But she did know the meaning of the words *pain and suffering, bleeding, and emotional upset* . . . and she did know the meaning of *sterility*. She was shocked and turned to show her father but realized it was useless. This was one word that truly frightened her and that needed clarification from the counselor.

VI. I realize that confidentiality may not be main-
tained in the event that complications requiring
hospitalization should occur.

VII. I agree that this consent to abortion shall be binding upon me and my heirs, executors and admin-
istrators.

VIII. I give this consent and certification of my own
free will and knowledge without force or coercion by another person(s).

She sighed deeply as she realized that force and coercion
were being used. But to fight it was useless.

She signed the consent form and continued to wait and secretly hope that something just might go wrong. It was the only
weapon she had left with which to fight her parents.

CHAPTER FOUR

The counseling session was brief but friendly. Debbie's counselor reviewed the information forms carefully and then asked if she had any questions.

"Is it possible that I may never be able to have another child?" inquired Debbie.

"Where in the world did you get that idea?"

"From one of your forms. It said that there might be pain and suffering and bleeding and sterility as a result of this abortion."

"Let me read part of the paragraph again to you, Debbie. It says that no one can completely guarantee the results of any surgery. There is always the possibility that something can go wrong. One of the very remote possibilities is sterility. In all my years of work in this clinic, I know of no one who has been made sterile by abortion. Our women are simply getting rid of some unwanted fetal matter just as they would get rid of some phlegm from their throat or mucous from their nose. The surgery is so simple and so painless that there is practically no chance of any complication whatever. That paragraph is for our protection in the unlikely event that something just might go wrong. I can assure you, Debbie, that nothing will happen. You'll feel a little sting from the needle when the anesthesia is given, you'll go to

25

sleep, the doctor will be finished in about ten minutes. You'll wake up to remember nothing that happened. You'll rest for a little while in the recovery room and then go home. You can go back to school tomorrow if you want to. You should plan to see your doctor in two weeks just to make sure you're okay. That's all there is to it. Does that answer your question, Debbie?"

"I think so, but what if I really don't want to have this abortion? Do I have to have it anyway?"

"No one can make that choice for you. I noticed that your mother and dad are with you. That's unusual. We seldom see a woman's parents in the clinic. You noted on the form that you were having this surgery because of parental pressure. Are they demanding that you have it?"

"Yes."

"They must have a good reason. Do you plan to live at home?"

"I really want to get married."

"And they want you to wait?"

"Yes—and they don't want me to marry Tim."

"And you really don't want this abortion?"

"I don't think so. I really don't know what I want. I—I just don't want to make waves, I guess. Tim doesn't have a job and we both have to finish high school and I don't want my folks to hate me. I suppose I'd just better go ahead and have the abortion."

"All right, then, we'll go ahead with the abortion."

Debbie's counselor showed her a diagram of the female reproductive system, pointed out the location of the uterus, and then with a pen traced the route of the egg down the fallopian tubes, where it joins with the male sperm.

"This is where conception takes place," she explained.

She laid the paper down, looked at Debbie, and said, "You are probably wondering just what this little blob looks like that the doctor is going to remove from your uterus today. It has practically no resemblance to anything human whatever and is no bigger than a peanut."

Debbie wanted to believe everything she was being told, but . . . somehow the thought of a little defenseless baby kept coming back to her. She tried to block it, to suppress it, to avoid it, even to redirect it, but the thought was there and it refused to leave.

When the counseling was finished, Debbie followed a nurse

through a single door into the room where the abortion was to take place.

The tile floor felt cold beneath her bare feet as she undressed behind a small screen. There was only a single hook on the wall where she hung all her clothes. As she had been directed, she put on a hospital gown, which came to mid-thigh and tied in the back. She then placed a small green bonnet, shaped like a shower cap, on her head.

Emerging from behind the screen, Debbie saw the nurse carefully arranging instruments on a towel. She looked away, but not before she had caught an unwanted glimpse of a number of stainless steel instruments, including a speculum, some forceps, and a set of different-sized dilators that were long and shaped like cigars. The sight of the instruments made her weak.

Using both hands to clutch her flimsy gown, Debbie made her way to the small table. She bumped against the long goose-necked lamp that stood against one end and moved around the metal stirrups that jutted out from the table. The stirrups gave the table the appearance of some medieval torture device. The nurse then moved a small stool to a spot nearby and directed Debbie to climb up.

The nurse scanned Debbie's medical history, then laid the forms aside.

"All right," she said, "let's get ready for the doctor. Lie down now and put your feet in the stirrups."

Debbie complied, unsuccessfully trying to hold the edges of her gown together. The metal stirrups felt like ice—and sent a chill through her entire body.

A freshly laundered sheet was draped over her body, and the nurse instructed Debbie to move down to the end of the table. Debbie used a sort of rotational movement of her hips and walked her backside toward her feet.

"A little more," the nurse said.

Debbie moved still farther down toward the stirrups until she felt like she was half off the end of the table.

"That's fine," said the nurse. "Now just relax until the doctor comes in."

"What a way to relax," thought Debbie. She had never felt so totally exposed . . . so completely vulnerable. She was already having second thoughts about this "simple, painless abortion procedure." She had suffered from just the embarrassment of the past few moments.

The anesthesiologist came in without knocking and pulled a stool up alongside the table near her left shoulder. He put a blood pressure cuff on one arm and then proceeded to wrap a tourniquet on the other between her elbow and shoulder.

Without looking at Debbie, he began to speak. "This tourniquet is going to feel tight like a rubber band for a few minutes," he said. "I need to put a small plastic needle into your arm. You'll feel a little pinch, a little sting, but it will stop very soon."

He probed the flesh until he located the vein. Debbie did feel "the pinch" and winced slightly.

"The fluid will feel cool as it runs up your vein," he added. He sounded totally detached from Debbie as he spoke. It was as though the whole procedure were just routine and terribly boring to him.

"You'll notice a garlic taste in your mouth as I begin to give you the sodium pentothol," he added. "The next thing you know you'll be awake and the surgery will be all over."

The anesthesiologist continued to talk until Debbie went completely limp. It took only a few seconds. He then placed a black rubber mask over her nose and mouth and carefully regulated the valve that dispensed the oxygen-enriched gas mixture that would assist her breathing and maintain the anesthetic during the brief surgery.

He constantly checked her heart rhythm and her blood pressure, and as always, he worried just a little. The risk factor wasn't high, but there was always the possibility that the surgical patient could vomit and pass the contents of the stomach into her lungs and cause a severe pneumonia. The patient's heart could stop as a result of the body's response to the gases or the unpredictable reflex activity as a result of the surgery. Debbie would never feel the pain caused by the dilation process, but the body responds anyway, and sometimes that response adversely affects the heart.

There's always the risk of malignant hyperthermia as the metabolism goes out of control. A patient's body temperature can rise as high as one-hundred-eight degrees very quickly. This reaction to the medication and drugs that are used is very rare but it does happen and when it does, a patient can die regardless of the emergency measures that are employed.

Debbie felt nothing. She remembered nothing. She didn't even see the surgeon before her abortion.

There was no memory of the trauma that took place for the next fifteen minutes.

She felt nothing as her legs were pulled up until her knees almost touched her stomach and then spread to their limit. She didn't feel the probing gloved fingers or the cold unfeeling speculum as it was thrust into her body.

The abortionist opened the speculum after he had inserted it and then visually examined the cervix and the neck of the womb.

The "sound," a long, slim measuring device, was then introduced into the uterus to determine its size and shape.

Debbie didn't feel the tremors that shook her body as the metallic, curved dilators were thrust through the opening to stretch the cervix.

The abortionist worked his way through the various graduated sizes until the cervix was sufficiently dilated to receive the suction apparatus.

The suction tube, about the size of a thick ball point pen, was taken from its sterile container and inserted through the dilated cervix up into the uterus, where it finally punctured the sac surrounding the child, allowing the amniotic fluid to escape.

For the first time, the instrument came in contact with the unborn child.

Neither Debbie, the abortionist, the anesthesiologist, nor the attending nurse were aware of the drama that was taking place just a few inches from each of them.

Completely hidden from view was an already fully developed baby, slightly less than twelve weeks old. Its head was cradled in the womb just as if it were being held in its mother's arms. Its body was stretched out, legs extended and moving, its hand resting against its face, thumb in its mouth. The orbit of the eyes was clearly discernible, the nose and mouth fully formed. If Debbie had viewed her "blob" through the technological magic of ultra-sound, she would also have seen the ventricle of the brain and a silhouette of the ribs and spine.

Its heart was beating at a measurable one-hundred-forty beats per minute.

As the surgery progressed, even Debbie was unaware of the

agitated movements of the child as it pulled itself away from the suction apparatus that had invaded the womb.

The heart rate sped up to over two hundred beats per minute as the child sensed the aggressive action of the abortionist.

As the sac was punctured and the fluid drained off, the suction tip was firmly clamped to the child's body. It was then pulled down by the suction device as pressure was applied to it. The body was being torn systematically piece by piece away from its head.

The violent defensive action of the child ceased.

The child's body was gone. All that remained were the head and fragments of the body.

The head was too large to be pulled in one piece by the suction tube. The abortionist employed a polyp forceps . . . grasped it tightly, crushed the head, and then removed the fractured pieces from the womb.

All that was left were small pieces of bone and strips of tissue that documented that these were the remains of what was once a living, unborn child.

As these pieces were finally sucked free of the womb, the abortion procedure was ended.

When Debbie finally woke up, it was just as she had been told. She remembered nothing. She was in a different room, on a little cot, and she was crying.

She felt her stomach and was surprised that it felt the same. She knew something was gone—something she hadn't wanted to lose—but she wasn't sure what it was or even how it had happened.

"Take these pills as directed," she was told. "They will prevent infection. You'll have some spotting and some cramping for a little while, but that will go away in a few hours."

"Go home, take it easy for the rest of the day. You'll be fine by tomorrow. Just be sure to have your doctor check you in two weeks."

Debbie was also given a twenty-one-day supply of birth control pills.

"She won't need those things," her mother said. "She won't be having any more sex until after she's married."

A nurse helped Debbie crawl into the back seat of her parents' car. She leaned her head against the cushion and tried to determine what it was that hurt.

There was discomfort and a little cramping, but there was something far deeper. It was an elusive emptiness that had invaded her whole being . . . it was a crushing feeling of total defeat in the only significant battle she'd ever fought . . . it was loss, the loss of the only thing she had ever really wanted to keep . . . it was distance, the gap, the wide, impossible gap that now had been built between a sixteen-year-old daughter and her parents.

"Well, that's over," her mother said. "Now you can start your life all over again."

Debbie was silent.

On the way home they stopped to pick up the family dog . . . a little brown and white terrier that had just had surgery for a small but aggravating hernia.

Debbie's dad placed the little dog in her arms and together a dog and a daughter whimpered in silent agony for the rest of the trip home.

CHAPTER FIVE

Nineteen months later, Tim and Debbie were married . . . in Seattle . . . secretly . . . in a civil ceremony.

Their dream had finally come true except that there was no little mobile home, just a one-bedroom flat with a bed, a table, two chairs, and a black and white television set. There was no motorcycle shop . . . just a job stocking shelves in a nearby grocery store. And there was no baby.

Debbie had found work as a nurse's aid in a local convalescent hospital.

The year-and-a-half period between the abortion and the wedding had been extremely difficult for both Tim and Debbie. Both of them lived at home, with parents, during that time. Both were heartsick—to the point of despair.

For six months, Debbie's menstrual cycle was interrupted. When it did resume, it was marked by such heavy bleeding that medical attention was required. A "strep" infection kept her out of school for two weeks. She developed a benign tumor in her right leg that eventually became so painful that surgical removal was necessary.

Each school year Debbie had prided herself on an almost absence-free attendance record. This year was a shambles. Every new illness was met with fear and bewilderment. She always questioned its relationship to the abortion and often wondered whether or not this was her punishment.

Her grade point average dropped from a near four point down to barely passing. She was removed from the scholastic society, forced to resign her office in the Junior Class, and dismissed from the school band. She locked her clarinet in its case, placed it under her bed, and never played it again.

Debbie lived in virtual silence with her parents. Their attempts to communicate were effectively resisted. She said nothing. She felt nothing but anger and deep resentment. That resentment grew into a full-blown bitterness that sank down deep into the core of Debbie's being and nibbled away at every sign of life that tried vainly to surface in the once-happy spirit of a vibrant teenager.

She stopped going to church completely. Thoughts of religion evoked only disgust. How could a Catholic mother be so active in the pro-choice movement? How could a Catholic father, who opposed abortion so violently, force his own daughter to abort an unborn baby?

Mr. Timms, her principal, had nothing to say to his long-time friend and neighbor.

Upon arriving home from school, she'd hang her coat in the hall closet, utter a lifeless "Hi," and go immediately to her room.

For hours she'd sit on her bed and look at the ever-changing scenes that framed themselves within the sills of her wide windows. She'd look at the distant hills that rose up from either side of the mighty Columbia, and then at the river itself as it made its way slowly, almost imperceptibly, from its source high in the Canadian Rockies down to its rendezvous with the Pacific Ocean 1200 miles downstream.

She'd look at the faraway mountain, her mountain, wrapped in its magnificent mantle of white, and marvel at its symmetry, its majesty. Days, weeks, could pass when Mt. Hood could be invisible . . . obscured completely by the clouds of rain and snow that shrouded it. Then suddenly, as if by magic, in a moment, it would reappear undisturbed, unperturbed, unchanged . . . as stately and as beautiful as ever.

Debbie had loved to study the changing colors of the sprawling apple and cherry orchards that blanketed the nearby hills. She would wonder at the ever-changing sky. She had studied the clouds and imagined all sorts of strange and wonderful creatures passing overhead.

This had been her world, her own wide, wonderful world, but now she looked at once-exciting scenes and saw nothing. A vast panorama of beauty was now dismal and ugly. Her world held no attraction; her life held no hope.

Debbie was finally forced to leave Jefferson and finish high school in a nearby community.

Tim had left home twice. His mother had found him with a loaded gun to his head and had seized it away from him before he could shoot himself. School had been impossible for him. He had lost his baby and his girl friend and had felt life hardly worth living.

They had communicated often, but always secretly. There were brief, unsatisfactory phone calls or little love notes slipped back and forth by friends. Occasionally they would catch a glimpse of each other, but they were never together, never alone until Debbie finally met Tim in Seattle.

Two weeks after the wedding, Debbie was pregnant. Both were ecstatic as they set up housekeeping in the tiny apartment.

As Debbie's pregnancy progressed, however, Tim began to withdraw. It was barely noticeable at first. Their lovemaking was less frequent. Tim became distant and detached. His work days grew longer, his periods at home shorter.

As they were watching television one evening, Debbie felt a slight movement in her womb and howled with delight. She took Tim's hand and tried to hold it on the very spot where she had detected life, but he jerked his hand back, got up, and walked away.

Tim was deeply disturbed and unable to explain why. Occasionally they would talk, but their conversations were always brief and usually unsatisfactory. They were both consumed with the problems of hard work, long hours, low pay, and too little time together.

Tim often mentioned the abortion. He seemed more concerned about the baby that was taken from them than the one they were about to have.

Debbie's expectancy gave way to apprehension as she

watched her husband's agitation increase. In a fit of anger, Tim struck Debbie—in the stomach—with his fist during a heated argument over finances and the ever-increasing medical bills. "I wish I had never met you, Deb," he shouted as he walked out the door. Debbie threw herself on the bed, holding her stomach, and sobbed.

An unexpected visit by her parents caught Debbie completely by surprise. She saw their car as it drew alongside the curb outside the apartment. Quickly she straightened the bed, placed the dirty dishes in the sink, and picked up clothes that were scattered around the room. Tim was at work, but the evidences of his presence were everywhere. Debbie's folks still didn't know about the wedding.

They had only been in the apartment a few minutes when Mrs. Porter spotted a man's sock under the bed. She drew it out, looked at it, and then at Debbie.

"Are you living with a guy?" she demanded.

"Yes. My husband lives here with me."

"Who is he?"

"Tim."

"How could you do this to us? We've told you he's no good! You'll never have anything if you live with that creep."

"We love each other."

"Love, love, what do you know about love? The only thing you two are after is sex. If you're not careful, you'll be pregnant again. Then what will you do?"

"I am pregnant again and we are going to have a baby."

"You're not going to have a baby. No child of mine is going to have a baby living in a dump like this and married to a no-good member of a motorcycle gang. You'll get another abortion, young lady, and you'll get it just as soon as you possibly can. You'll get an abortion or we won't have anything to do with you."

"Then you'll have nothing to do with me!" shouted Debbie. "Now, will you please leave and don't you ever come here again."

Debbie's parents left. When Tim returned from work, he found his wife sitting limply in a chair, too tired to move, too drained to even cry.

In July, Jennifer was born. Five days later, Tim left for work and never returned. A brief note arrived a week later. Debbie unfolded it and read it with trembling hands. It said:

I'm sorry, Deb. We couldn't have the baby we wanted and now we've got one that I can't stand. It's too much for me to handle.

Tim

Debbie never saw Tim again.

CHAPTER SIX

Debbie counted out fifteen benedrils . . . all she had left from a previous prescription . . . and swallowed them along with a bottle of wine. She got sleepy, slightly drunk, and terribly sick. She vomited until she felt there was nothing left inside of her. She found an old bottle of phenobarbitol. There were only five pills. She took them all and again experienced only violent nausea.

In desperation, she threw two wine bottles into the sink, picked up a shard of broken glass, and slashed at her wrist and elbow. She saw the blood as it began to drain from her body. She looked at the tendons and the fat clearly visible through the torn skin. She watched with silent fascination as the white porcelain turned red and little spots of blood began to spatter on the faucet and the drainboard.

Jennifer woke up, crying as usual.

Without a moment's hesitation, Debbie grabbed a dish towel from the sink, fixed a tourniquet around her left arm, called a neighbor to watch the baby, and rushed off to a doctor.

"I was trying to put up a window and the glass slipped and fell against my arm," she explained.

The doctor believed her as he silently sutured two jagged and ugly wounds.

Debbie and Jennifer moved to Hood River, back to her

parents' home . . . a great place to live, but the last place in all the world she wanted to be.

It was a brief respite. The relationship was intolerable. Debbie took her baby back to Seattle, hired a baby sitter, and went to work again as a nurses' aid.

The days were long, the work was hard, and the pay was low. Her greatest frustration was that she never had the energy to enjoy her daughter. At night, when they were together, Debbie was irritable and sleepy, and Jennifer was always demanding attention that Debbie did not want to give.

For $2.65 an hour, Debbie was forced to leave home at 5:00 A.M., walk two miles, mostly uphill, spend eight and a half hours caring for the sick, and then walk back home again. In the evenings she'd carry Jennifer and the laundry three blocks to a laundromat, return home, clean the apartment, prepare meals for the next day, press her clothes, and search vainly for a few sane moments to relax.

It was bad enough when Jennifer was well. When she developed a chronic ear infection along with her never-ending colic, it became impossible. Two-year-old Jennifer needed a mother, but Debbie needed money. To provide both was impossible. When medicines were needed, Debbie became desperate. There was no way she could meet all the demands that were being placed upon her.

Tim's mother, now widowed and living in Seattle, called one evening. They talked for a long time. Virginia had seen little of Debbie and Jennifer since her son had left them. She was lonesome for her only granddaughter, and after hearing of Debbie's problem, she offered to keep Jennifer for a weekend.

Debbie spent Saturday and Sunday catching up on her many neglected projects. She even found some spare time to rest. On Monday she called Virginia and asked if she could keep Jennifer a little longer.

Virginia was delighted. "I'll keep this little doll forever if you'll let me," she replied.

On Wednesday, Virginia called and advised Debbie that Jennifer needed medical attention.

"I'll be right over," Debbie said quickly.

"Oh, you don't need to come, Debbie. I can handle this. I've got a car and Jennifer and I can drive over to the clinic first thing in the morning. I do have a problem, though. If Jennifer needs much medication or care, I really don't have the money. I was just reading through my medical policy and there's no way that I can have Jennifer's bills absorbed by it, even though she's my grand-daughter. There is one possibility. A friend, who is a lawyer, told me this morning that if I am given temporary legal custody of the child, then all her bills will be paid by my insurance."

"Really?" said Debbie. "It's as simple as that? Are you really willing to do something like that, Virginia?"

"Certainly. I'll drive over tonight and you can sign these papers. I can take Jennifer to the clinic in the morning, and then when you want her released from my custody, you can have her, no questions asked," said Virginia.

On the same day Debbie released Jennifer to her mother-in-law, she met Mike. They were waiting for the same bus, headed in the same direction, and lived in the same area.

Mike was ruggedly handsome, with dark wavy hair and flashing brown eyes. He was dressed in slacks and a short-sleeved shirt that emphasized his broad chest, wide shoulders, and muscled arms. He was a national wrestling champion and now worked in a North Seattle clinic as a medical aid.

They were immediately attracted to each other through their similar professions, but there was more. There was an easiness in Mike's manner and an attentiveness in Mike's eyes. Debbie found herself talking to someone who seemed to be listening for a change.

This was the first night in months that Debbie didn't have to hurry home. Jennifer was in good care . . . tomorrow was her day off . . . and she suddenly found herself delightfully relaxed. They sat at the bus stop and watched three Aurora Street buses go by before making any attempt to move.

"Let's go up to the Space Needle for a drink," Mike suggested.

"Sure, why not," Debbie replied. "Do you realize that I've been in this city for a whole year and haven't been up in the Space Needle yet?"

The city was just settling into its night clothes as they walked briskly from the bus stop down Pine Street to the Westlake Mall, where they caught the Monorail to Seattle's famous Space Needle.

They chatted endlessly as they moved through the turnstile, into the elevator, and then up 500 feet to an observation platform that encircled the entire structure.

Debbie had never seen Seattle from this vantage point before. Her eyes widened and her speech slowed as she began to take in the sights of the magnificent city sprawled beneath them.

The western sky, tinted pink from the lowering sun, was casting its colors on the sprawling Olympic Range that lifted from the Peninsula far beyond the expansive waters of Puget Sound.

She watched as ferries, headed for Bremerton, jockeyed back and forth among the oceangoing ships and then docked at the fingerlike piers that jutted out into Elliott Bay from what appeared to be the very heart of downtown Seattle.

Land reached up and stretched out in every direction into the waters beneath her. "The Indians believed that Puget Sound and its many islands were created by the Great Spirit simply because he loved beautiful things," Mike explained.

To the South, she saw the central business district dotted with thirty- to fifty-story office buildings.

"This Space Needle was built in 1962," Mike said. "Seattle was then hosting the World's Fair. At the time it was built, it was the tallest structure in town.

"Do you see that little needlelike spire barely visible through the buildings . . . the one that looks like a miniature Empire State Building?" He moved Debbie just slightly until the almost invisible tower came into view. "That building," he explained, "is the old L. C. Smith Tower. It used to be the first tall building one would see as he came within sight of Seattle from across the Sound. People here used to brag that the Smith Tower was the tallest building west of the Mississippi. Now even the Space Needle is dwarfed by some of the new skyscrapers."

As they walked to their left, Debbie looked down nearly a tenth of a mile to the street lights that were just beginning to flicker on, and the twin dots from automobile headlights that were inching their way through the heavily trafficked streets that ran parallel to the waterfront.

A helicopter passed beneath them, its strobe light piercing the approaching darkness. It descended slowly and then hovered for just a brief moment before settling on its landing pad atop a nearby newspaper building.

The silhouette of Mount Rainier loomed up in the distant sky. Debbie watched as its nearly three-mile-high tip turned from light pink to white and then to gray and finally to black as it went through its evening ritual of bidding goodnight to its millions of admirers.

Mike pointed out the Cascades to the east . . . a range of mountains that included Debbie's own Mount Hood to the south, Mount St. Helens, Mount Rainier, and Mount Baker visible in the far northern sky.

"That string of mountains is one of the greatest ranges of mountains in the West," Mike said. "It stretches from the Sierra Nevadas in Central California, all the way up through the States of Oregon and Washington and on into the southern tip of British Columbia. Many of the peaks are extinct or active volcanoes."

Mike pointed out Lake Washington, the campus of the University, and Lake Union, oftentimes called the City's Backdoor. Its fresh-water harbor was surrounded by warehouses, railroad lines, trucking companies, and giant cranes that never seemed to rest from their industrial frenzy.

They looked down at Queen Anne Hill. "That's where the City had its beginning," he said. "Behind that little hill is a canal with a series of locks that makes it possible to travel by boat from the salt water of Elliott Bay in Puget Sound, up through Lake Union's fresh water to Lake Washington. You can actually tie up right alongside the University campus if you want to."

Debbie watched the natural splendor as the shadows descended over the city and then saw them give way to a spectacle of lights that spread for miles in every direction. She stood in silence, trying to print each one of the thousand different scenes on her mind.

They finally moved to the elevator and down to the lounge. They continued to watch as their place in the sky moved slowly through its 360-degree arc. Each time they looked, they saw something new . . . something different . . . until their minds drifted back to themselves and they found themselves again absorbed with each other.

The world around them was soon forgotten. They talked about everything: music and sports and medicine and their families. Debbie told Mike about Tim and Jennifer and that her divorce was almost final.

Mike had been married and had two children . . . he now lived alone. He described an unhappy marriage with a woman who didn't understand him and who had finally left him for another man.

Debbie couldn't remember ever being happier. They left the lounge hand in hand, completely oblivious to the fast-paced world around them. Debbie wasn't even aware of the quick elevator descent to the ground. She was only conscious of Mike.

"You're too good a woman to live alone," Mike said as they seated themselves in the rear of one of Seattle's articulated Metro buses. "When your divorce is final, will you marry me, Debbie?"

"But, Mike, we just met" . . . she looked quickly at her watch . . . "three hours and fifteen minutes ago. I hardly know you."

"Love is not a slave to time," Mike answered. "I feel I have known you a lifetime. In these past three hours we've been up to heaven, we've traveled around the world three times, we've shared all the major events of two lifetimes, and our hearts have learned to speak to each other. How many people have lived together for their whole lives and have never shared as much as we have in just 195 minutes?"

Debbie lifted her head to kiss him lightly on the cheek. "Yes, Mike," she said. "I will marry you."

CHAPTER SEVEN

It seemed so right to Debbie that she and Mike should live together. That decision was made within just a few days of their introduction.

Mike moved in to Debbie's little one-room apartment, strung a light-weight rope from one corner of the room to another, then draped it with a flimsy bedspread. They both felt awkward making love in the presence of a little child.

Each morning they would leave for work early. Debbie would drive Mike in his car and then leave Jennifer with her grandmother.

At two, Jennifer was a beautiful child. Her silky, light brown hair and sparkling blue eyes were much like Debbie's had been at that age. She was alert, learning to explore with all sorts of strange sounds and little words and was into everything. The unending responsibilities of a new mother only increased as the child grew. Debbie loved her daughter, but since she had met Mike, she began sensing an ever-increasing desire to be free. She found herself becoming less patient. Short tempered. And there were times when that anger exploded into abuse.

Striking a two-year-old? Such a thing would have been unthinkable to Debbie at an earlier period in her life. Now it was becoming routine.

Mike and Debbie began leaving her alone with greater frequency. Often they'd return late at night to a crying child and a complaining neighbor.

Virginia noticed the frightening changes that were taking place. Occasionally she'd see little welts on her granddaughter's body and she'd sense fear in the little girl's eyes.

Debbie was always in a hurry, and each morning now she'd leave her daughter still dressed in her night clothes, often without her breakfast. Only seldom would she even take the time to tell Jennifer good-bye.

Virginia knew nothing about Mike.

Virginia, who had recently remarried, asked one Monday morning, "Why don't you leave Jennifer all week? It's so far to drive each day. Henry and I are all alone here . . . we have all the room we need, and she seems to be so happy with us."

"Would you mind?" asked Debbie. "I haven't been feeling well lately and I'm so tired all the time. Maybe in a few days I'll feel more like taking care of her."

"Leave her with us. Get yourself some rest. We'll take good care of her; in fact, we'll have fun together."

Debbie lifted Jennifer into her arms and asked, "Would you like to stay with Grandma?" The little two-year-old twisted away from her mother and stretched an arm in the direction of Grandma—wiggling until Debbie put her down. "I guess that answers that question," she said.

The young mother appeared reluctant to leave, but inwardly Debbie could hardly wait to get out the door and down the front steps to the car and back to the apartment where Mike was waiting.

Both had called in to work sick that day. They spent the morning hours alone, secluded, in private . . . the first privacy they had known since they met. They ate, dressed, and climbed into Mike's old car to go for a drive. They had no plans, no destination, just the urge to go.

Together they drove the streets of Seattle, looked at its sights, and talked unendingly. They walked through the winding paths of Woodland Park and visited the zoo. They saw all sorts of things that day, animals, rivers, lakes, mountains, ships, magnificent structures, and historic sites, but they remembered very little.

They were consumed with each other. They talked about their past, but even more about their future. They dreamed of all sorts of wedding plans from the smallest, most private to the most elaborate ceremony they could think of.

Debbie even considered a church wedding . . . a Catholic church wedding. She loved the thoughts of a gown, a veil, flowers, attendants, and beautiful music. She wanted the blessing of her priest, the presence of her parents, the excitement of a crowd. She had missed all of these with Tim. It would be just like starting over again and maybe this time . . . it would work.

Mike said little but listened intently to the excited ramblings of the woman beside him. Both were convinced that their lives were just beginning and that the past with all of its haunting memories would now be buried forever.

The realities of life would crash into their dream world with frightening regularity. Every day would begin with the high-pitched buzzing of an alarm that would force them to disentangle their bodies and move from the cozy warmth of their bed to the cold, disinterested world that continued to make impossible demands of them.

They never had quite enough money for Mike to pay child support, nor quite enough gas to go where they wanted, nor quite enough food to eat as they wished, nor quite enough room to live in comfort, nor quite enough furniture to sprawl in ease, nor quite enough clothes to dress as they pleased, nor quite enough time to say and do all the things they wanted.

Jennifer consumed their weekends. From Friday night until Monday morning, their life was one continuous interruption that soon turned into a continual frustration. Frustration became irritation and irritation became anger and all the pent-up anger was directed at an innocent and uncomprehending little child. Jennifer became silent. Her little, unrecognizable sounds ceased. Her eyes lost their sparkle. Her actions were measured and slow. Her head was usually bowed, her cheeks limp in a little pout, and her finger constantly pressed between her front teeth.

It was no problem whatever to Debbie to leave Jennifer with her grandmother. She only wished at times that she could leave her forever.

Both divorces were proceeding slowly. Tim could not be located and Mike's wife was making impossible demands.

Debbie discovered she was pregnant. She had been taking the pill faithfully until she could stand the headache and dizziness no longer. She had marked her calendar with care. She and Mike had been particularly cautious during the days of her fertility. Nevertheless, Debbie was pregnant.

Mike changed. The loving, sensitive, intensely interested, satisfying lover became an angry, sullen, detached man. A wild man.

He demanded that Debbie have an abortion . . . immediately. "I will not have another baby . . . now or ever," he shouted. "You've got one that I can't stand and I've got two I can't afford."

"Anything you say, Mike. I'll get an abortion. I've had one. I can't see that another one will make any difference."

"And get rid of that kid."

"But Mike, Jennifer is my daughter."

"I don't care," said Mike. "I can't stand that bawling kid any longer. If you want to live with me, Debbie, you'll have to get rid of Jennifer."

"Anything you say, Mike." Debbie couldn't bear the thought of losing Mike. For the first time in her life she had felt wanted. She had dreamed. She had loved and she had been loved. These few months had been the best she'd ever known and she wanted them to last forever.

Mike was transferred to Spokane. Debbie made plans to follow. She took Jennifer to Virginia's the following Monday, left a small suitcase filled with clothes and toys, said goodbye, and headed downtown . . . not to work, but to the Planned Parenthood Office to make arrangements for her second abortion.

Debbie had no intention of returning that night or that weekend to pick up her little girl.

CHAPTER EIGHT

The people at Planned Parenthood were friendly as usual. They confirmed Debbie's pregnancy with a simple urine test and encouraged her to get an abortion. They only hesitated when Debbie asked them to pay for it.

"But I don't have any money," Debbie complained.

"I'm sorry," she was told, "but we aren't in the business of financing abortions. We are a counseling agency, and it's only under the most unusual circumstances that emergency funding is available."

"Wouldn't *this* be an emergency situation? I'm nearly twelve weeks pregnant, my husband has left me, and our divorce is not final. My boyfriend has moved away. I have a two-year-old daughter that I can't support. My job pays $2.65 an hour, and all of that goes to pay for food and rent. My folks won't help me. I don't dare tell them that I've been living with another guy."

Debbie was finally given forms to apply for Title Twenty funding, filled them out, and returned to her little apartment to wait for an answer.

For three days she waited. Each morning she would walk to the corner, deposit twenty-five cents in a pay phone, and call Planned Parenthood. Each time she would get the same reply, "Sorry, your request for funding is still being considered. We're unable to give you a decision as yet."

Debbie was very much aware of her pregnancy. Her clothes were tight and her stomach felt bloated. She had been sick each morning from the beginning and was ravenously hungry.

The whole process would be fairly simple, she'd thought. After Mike left, she had planned to quit her job, leave Jennifer with Virginia, have the abortion, and then take the bus to Spokane to join Mike as soon as possible.

She had quit her job. She had left Jennifer, but the abortion process was being delayed. For three days she sat in her empty apartment and waited.

She blocked Jennifer out of her mind. She blocked the abortion process from her thinking, but she couldn't forget Mike. Debbie was desperately lonely.

On the fourth day, she was informed that her Title Twenty funding request had been approved. She was to pick up the forms and take them Monday morning at nine o'clock to the Sixth Avenue Medical Clinic.

Debbie was awakened late Saturday morning by an insistent knock. She jumped out of bed and ran to the door fully expecting Mike. As she reached for the latch, she froze. *What if it's Virginia?*

Through the window she saw Virginia's car and knew that her mother-in-law and her daughter were standing outside the door. She could have bluffed her way through this encounter easily, but her mind went blank. She crouched in a far corner and waited until the knocking ceased. She then listened to the uncertain footsteps of her little girl walking down the creaking stairs to the street below. Debbie watched them as they climbed into the car and drove away.

On Sunday, she reread the instruction forms in preparation for her Monday morning abortion.

1. Unless you are a diabetic, please do not eat breakfast or drink any liquids.

That will be hard, she thought.

2. If possible, bring someone with you.

That will be impossible. She only had Mike and he was in Spokane.

3. Take a bath or a shower before you come for your appointment and wear only light-weight clothing. Avoid tight clothing or turtleneck sweaters.

Debbie could understand the request to not wear tight clothing, but why not a turtleneck sweater?

4. When you come to the Clinic the following tests will be done: RH, blood grouping, urinalysis, and another pregnancy test.

Another pregnancy test? That sure wouldn't be necessary.

5. Our fee is $200. We will accept the fee in cash, money order, or a cashier's check. We do not accept personal checks.

There it was again, Debbie thought. The same statement that had been read to her father in the Hood River Clinic. She relived the embarrassment of that encounter and reached for the Title Twenty form to be certain that she would not be denied an abortion for lack of funds.

6. If you think your insurance will cover the abortion, you should pay us the total $200 and have your insurance company reimburse you. We will be glad to give you an itemized statement for this purpose and/or help you fill out the necessary insurance forms.
7. Please call us if you will not be able to keep your appointment. We have many women waiting for appointment schedules.

Debbie had no plans to miss this appointment.

The information sheet then reminded her that she should plan to spend two to three hours at the Clinic and that a counselor would discuss all of her options with her. She would also receive written and oral instructions before leaving, and she should remain for at least one half hour following the abortion procedure.

Debbie didn't allow herself the privilege of thinking . . . she didn't dare. She would never forget the anger, the fear, the uncertainty, and the complications of her first abortion, but she could not allow those thoughts to surface.

Abortion was legal. Abortion was safe. Abortion was a rational choice. Abortion was quick and simple. This was the limit of her reasoning. This was the extent of her thinking. This was all she allowed. Debbie effectively ruled out any other thoughts until she found herself forced to wait in the Sixth Avenue Medical Clinic seven interminable hours for her abortion to take place.

From nine in the morning until four in the afternoon Debbie waited and Debbie fumed and Debbie . . . read. She read every magazine, every paper, and every pamphlet she could lay her hands on.

She wished she hadn't. Too many of the pro-choice, pro-abortion pamphlets listed the arguments of the pro-life people.

She was especially interested in a folder entitled, "Catholics Speak Out for the Right to Choose Abortion."[1]

"Seventy-nine percent of American Catholics," the article stated, "believe in abortion rights." Debbie became increasingly uneasy as she read. The folder supported a woman's right to choose—but it didn't always seem to support abortion. A statement by Congressman Mickey Leland of Texas read, "As a Catholic, I personally consider abortion to be a serious moral problem. The decision to terminate a pregnancy is a question of conscience and undoubtedly a personal matter. I would vote against any legislation that would hinder any woman from expressing her freedom of choice."

A question of conscience . . . a personal matter . . . freedom of choice . . . Debbie had no problem with those statements. It was statements like these that had prompted her decision. But when she read words such as ". . . a serious moral problem" she felt uncomfortable. "It doesn't really *sound* like he's a Catholic in favor of abortion," she thought.

She read further. Judge John Dosling—another Catholic— had said, "A woman's conscientious decision in consultation with her physician to terminate her pregnancy because it is medically necessary to her health is an exercise of the most fundamental of rights, nearly allied to her right to be."

"I agree," thought Debbie . . . but then she studied it further. He said that the decision was to be made in consultation with a physician and he assumed that abortion was designed to

---

1. "Catholics Speak Out for the Right to Choose Abortion," published by Catholics for a Free Choice, 2008 17th St. N. W., Washington, D. C. 20009.

terminate a pregnancy because it was medically necessary. "I haven't talked to a doctor," she said to herself. "I've only seen the people at Planned Parenthood; and I'm not sick. This abortion is for Mike. I can't have a baby and Mike, too, and I want Mike. It's that simple."

A picture of Congresswoman Geraldine Ferraro of New York, another Catholic, was placed alongside one of her statements: "This country is based on a separation of Church and State. As a Catholic I accept the premise that a fertilized ovum is a baby. I have been blessed with the gift of faith but others have not. I have no right to impose my beliefs on them."

Debbie was startled. She reread the sentence which said, "I accept the premise that a fertilized ovum is a baby." That was what she had thought. That was what her priest had said. That was what her dad had said. It was Planned Parenthood and her counselor in the Hood River Clinic who had said that it was just an accumulation of cells or a mass of impersonal protoplasm.

A statement by Father Richard McBrien read, "If, after appropriate study, reflection and prayer, a person is convinced that his or her conscience is correct, in spite of a conflict with the moral teachings of the Church, the person not only may, but must, follow the dictates of conscience rather than the teachings of the Church."

"I haven't studied," thought Debbie. "And I sure haven't prayed. And I'm not about to do either. Just reading these things makes me confused. If I prayed . . . if I prayed . . . what if God told me not to get an abortion?" Debbie couldn't handle that possibility.

She picked up another pamphlet. This one began: "You Know Them As the 'Right to Life' People. They Oppose Abortion. But Did You Know . . .

> . . . that they are against contraception?
> . . . that they oppose sex education in the schools?
> . . . that they are working to stop research in amniocentesis, the science of detecting prenatal birth defects?
> . . . that they helped persuade Congress to deny poor women access to abortions?"[2]

---

2. Naral Foundation, 825 15th St. N.W., Washington, D. C. 20005.

As she read further, she noted that the "Right to Life" people were out to force an amendment to the Constitution banning abortions under any circumstances, that these people would employ any means—even lies—to stop abortions, and that a pregnant woman must have her baby whether she wants it or not.

That was a little too much for Debbie. As far as keeping her baby was concerned . . . she would have loved that. But that would mean giving up Mike.

She read pamphlets entitled, "This Issue Is Freedom, Not Abortion," "The Supreme Court and Reproductive Freedom," "The Hyde Amendment . . . An ASSAULT ON THE MORAL INTEGRITY OF THE POOR," and others. Most of the arguments seemed based on emotion, not reason. All of them stressed freedom of choice and the legality of abortion.

Debbie was not sure that these were the only arguments. She grappled with the presence of a human life in her body and she wrestled with something way down deep . . . a gnawing, restless something that wouldn't seem to go away. She remembered hearing her priest say that "legality is not the ultimate criterion . . . Jesus was legally crucified."

She watched the hands of the large clock on the far wall. They seemed to be motionless. This was the longest day in Debbie's life . . . a day she had tried carefully to avoid . . . a day she was forced to think and rethink, to consider what it was she was about to do.

The waiting room was empty when her name was finally called.

There was the routine counseling session, a description of the process of pregnancy, and a few words about the method of abortion. She would have only a local anesthetic this time and would be awake during the entire procedure. Methods of birth control were explained again and there was some mention of options.

When she was given an opportunity for questions, Debbie had only one.

"Is this a live baby in me?"

"What the doctor is removing from you today is a fetus," the counselor answered. "It's an accumulation of cells, with very little resemblance to anything human."

Debbie was told to undress from the waist down, and then

to climb up on the small table with the ever-present stirrups.

The doctor was very kind. He held Debbie's hand and asked if she had any questions. She asked the question again. The question that smoldered and threatened to leap into flame.

"Is there a live baby in me?"

"If there is anything living in you," he answered, "its spirit will be passed on to your next baby."

Debbie relaxed . . . still confused . . . but there was no other option as far as she was concerned.

She felt the initial pelvic exam and then the insertion of the cold, steel speculum. A gonorrhea culture was taken and placed on the nearby counter. She felt the pressure from the next instrument as it gripped the mouth of her uterus and then the sting of the needle as the carbocaine was injected into the cervix to deaden it.

Within seconds Debbie began to feel light-headed and a little dizzy. There was a slight ringing in her ears and her mouth felt dry.

The cramps were almost unbearable as the cervix was enlarged by the insertion of the dilators, and then she heard the low hum of an electric motor as it was turned on.

Something began tugging and pulling in her lower abdomen. The cramps reminded her of the labor pains she had felt when Jennifer was born. She bit her lip and tightened her grip against the table and tried to keep from crying but couldn't. It hurt . . . it hurt bad. Oh, how she wished for the money for a general anesthetic.

"We're almost finished," the doctor said. "Almost finished . . . almost finished . . . there! That's all there is to it. That wasn't so bad now, was it?"

Debbie was perspiring, tears were rolling down the sides of her head and piling up in her ears. Her mouth was too dry to speak and her whole body still shaking from the cramps and the tension of the past few minutes.

She was given codeine for pain, another twenty-one days' supply of contraceptive pills, and a sanitary napkin to absorb the flow of blood.

After resting, Debbie dressed, and then walked to a nearby Burger King and ate two large hamburgers.

It was eight weeks before she was able to leave Seattle. She bled constantly, passed large clots, and developed an infection that caused a foul-smelling, green discharge. She was forced to change pads constantly to keep the blood from ruining her clothes.

The Planned Parenthood people refused to fund medical attention or a prescription.

A Catholic Hospital finally diagnosed her bladder and kidney infection as Trichimonis, and told her it could have been caused by non-sterile instruments. They gave her a prescription for Flagyl.

Debbie stayed in her tiny apartment, refused to answer her door, and tried to keep herself alive with the meager food supply she had available.

As soon as she was able, she packed her little suitcase, walked to the edge of the city, and began hitch-hiking east to Spokane.

She found Mike's apartment and Mike dressed only in his trousers, drinking a can of beer . . . with another woman.

There was no explanation; there was no apology; there was no invitation even to come in. Debbie just stood there in the open door, trying to sort through the impact of what she was seeing. She took a step backwards, turned, and walked back out onto the street with absolutely no idea of what she would do next.

CHAPTER NINE

It really wasn't too hard for Debbie to find another man.

Ken picked her up about twenty miles west of Spokane while she was hitch-hiking, and drove her all the way back to Seattle. Of course she had to pay him for the ride, but there were ways for Debbie to show her gratitude to a man, even when she had no money. She had learned them well.

It really wasn't too hard for Debbie to find a job.

Seattle is filled with convalescent hospitals and retirement homes looking for experienced help willing to work for a minimum wage.

It really wasn't too hard for Debbie to find a place to live.

Ken's little apartment was big enough for both. Ken was no substitute for Mike, but he was company and he provided a place to sleep and someone to talk to . . . when he wasn't drunk.

It really wasn't too hard for Debbie to get pregnant again. She had long since used up her twenty-one-day supply of pills, and since her second abortion, her periods had been totally unpredictable.

It really wasn't too hard to predict Ken's reaction to Debbie's pregnancy.

Rejection, she had expected. It was the violence of that rejection that took her by surprise. Ken slapped Debbie, kicked her, pushed her down two flights of apartment house stairs, and then threw her clothes down after her.

What was hard for Debbie was to see Jennifer again. It took two weeks to recover from the injuries sustained from her abusive boyfriend. As soon as she was able, Debbie went to Virginia's to see Jennifer. It had been seven months since she had heard her daughter's footsteps in the apartment hallway . . . seven months since she had seen her drive away with her grandmother . . . seven months and she had made no contact whatever.

Debbie was not allowed inside Virginia's house. She was forbidden the privilege of seeing her own child. Virginia advised her that the temporary custody papers Debbie had signed months before were legal and binding, and that she had been reporting Debbie's "outrageous" conduct through her attorney to the court.

"Henry and I are ready to initiate proceedings to gain full custody of Jennifer," Virginia told her, "and I really doubt that there is anything you can do about it." With that, she slammed the front door in Debbie's face.

A room in the YWCA was more than she could afford, but it was all that was available. Debbie sat alone staring at four bare walls and watching the flimsy curtains blow back and forth in the breeze from the open window.

She looked down at the street six floors below and wondered just how it would feel to jump . . . to fall . . . to hit. There were other methods to take her life, but they were all too messy or too painful. She had no drugs available for an overdose.

On the top of an old chest of drawers she spotted a Gideon Bible. It had been years since she'd held her Catholic Bible in her hands. She hadn't been able to understand it then and probably couldn't understand it any better now.

Debbie decided that the only place in all the world where she might find a friend was back again at the Planned Parenthood Center. She talked to a counselor about Jennifer and was referred to a nearby legal aid office.

It was extremely difficult to answer the questions that were asked of her. It wasn't that she didn't know the answers, the problem was that she couldn't believe that this was her life that was being unfolded before her.

"Let me see if I've got this straight," the attorney said. "You were forced by your parents to have an abortion when you were sixteen. You married at eighteen, had a daughter nine months later, and then your husband left you. That divorce became final only six months ago. You became pregnant by a man who was not your husband and had that pregnancy terminated by an abortion, and now you're pregnant again by another man to whom you're not married. You left your daughter with your mother-in-law, who has a legal document giving her temporary custody, and now she won't give your child back to you.

"How long has it been since you last saw your child?"

"Seven months."

"Have you made any attempt to see her in that time?"

"Yes, I tried to see her yesterday."

"Was that the only time you have tried to see her?"

"Yes."

"Why didn't you see her? Were you out of town or out of the country?"

"No, except for just a few days."

"Did you try to communicate with her in any other way . . . by phone or by letter?"

"No."

"Why didn't you?"

Debbie was afraid that this question would be asked, and she really didn't know how to answer it. If she told the truth, it might mean she'd never see Jennifer again. She thought for a few minutes, dropped her head, and feebly said, "I don't know."

"The courts usually rule in favor of a mother having custody of her own child," the attorney explained, "but I really can't tell you what they might decide in your case. There is one thing for certain. If you petition the court to regain legal custody of your child and then show up in the courtroom unmarried and pregnant, it sure isn't going to help your case any. I'd advise you to have another abortion as soon as you possibly can."

"Isn't there any other way besides abortion?" Debbie asked.

"I don't know of any," he answered. "At least I don't know of any that might give you a chance to recover your child."

Her third abortion was scheduled at the Sixth Avenue Medical Clinic again, and again it was financed by Title Twenty funding. The Planned Parenthood people were not particularly happy to extend help to Debbie this time, and she found that many of her calls were not being returned and most of her requests were being denied.

It was no longer necessary for Debbie to be told what to do. She filled out the forms, listened again to the counselor, took off her clothes, climbed on the table, and scooted her body as far down as it would go.

The procedure was similar but not the same. She was given a local anesthetic as before, but this time rather than a probing suction tube, there was the intrusion of a long, sharp knife called a curette. After the dilation process had taken place, the surgeon then cut the placenta and the baby into pieces and scraped the pieces out into a basin.

During the entire abortion, Debbie was screaming to the abortionist to stop. At six weeks, she was certain that this would be the simplest and least painful, but it hurt far more than before.

She could feel the scraping and the pulling, and each time she screamed, the abortionist would say, "We can't stop now. It'll be over in just a minute. We can't stop now."

"I can feel it," Debbie cried. "It hurts. Can't you give me something . . . anything for the pain?"

"It'll be all over in just a minute," was the only thing he would say.

Before the abortionist was finished, he inserted a plastic IUD (Intrauterine Device) into Debbie's uterus. The people at Planned Parenthood had recommended this and had offered to pay the bill. Debbie had agreed.

They had told her that an IUD inserted by a doctor or a nurse practitioner would almost guarantee that she would not become pregnant as long as it remained in place. An IUD actually prevents the egg from being implanted in the wall of the uterus. It might cause heavier than usual menstrual bleeding and it could cause some possible cramping, but since it would relieve anxiety over pregnancy, it could improve sexual relations considerably.

Debbie wasn't altogether sure about sexual relations, but she was certain that she wanted no more pregnancies.

After the abortion, Debbie passed large clots of blood that looked like pieces of liver, and two weeks later she expelled a thick piece of gauze about two inches square that had evidently been left in her uterus.

She experienced constant pain. It hurt to ride on a bus or in a car. Her call to Planned Parenthood went unanswered for two days. When she did finally reach her counselor, she was told never to call them again.

CHAPTER TEN

Three weeks later Debbie met Steve. She wasn't the least bit interested in him—or any other man. She was fed up with men and concerned about changing her life.

But Steve was different. She studied him carefully the night they met at a girl friend's house. He was about five-foot-eight, had brown hair, a neatly trimmed beard, and wore glasses. She was impressed by his muscular build, but even more taken with his quiet manner.

Steve was a structural engineer at Boeing Aircraft Company and did most of his work on computers.

Debbie agreed to let him drive her home in his red Camaro. They stopped for pizza on the way. A few days later he popped into her newly rented apartment just to say hi. He made no advances, no demands. He never touched her.

Debbie had been unable to make her rent payment. She owed $200. She was sitting on her bed trying to figure some way to pay it, when Steve arrived.

"I'll pay it," he said. "I'd be glad to pay it for you, Debbie."

"Steve, you can't do that. I could never repay you."

"Sure, I can do that, and you don't need to repay me."

"But, Steve," Debbie emphasized clearly and carefully, "there is no possible way I can ever repay you."

"Debbie," Steve said emphatically, "there is no way you will ever be asked to repay me. No way whatsoever!"

Debbie began to cry. "You mean you are willing to do this for me . . . just for me . . . and for no other reason?"

"That's right, Debbie . . . just for you and for no other reason."

Steve counted out one hundred and sixty dollars, laid it on the kitchen table, told Debbie good night, and left.

Steve and Debbie's relationship wasn't particularly exciting, but it was very comfortable and peaceful.

There was no attempt at any sexual encounter. Debbie couldn't have performed sexually if she had wanted to; the pain was too severe and it was constant.

Debbie went to church with Steve. It was her first time in a Protestant Church. She had never heard such enthusiastic singing nor had she listened to a sermon that she could fully understand. She was somewhat perplexed by it all, but as she and Steve had lunch together, she was forced to admit that she did enjoy it . . . a little bit anyway.

Two young women from Steve's church called at Debbie's apartment the following week. They stated very plainly that they had come to talk with her about her personal relationship with Jesus Christ.

"I'm a Christian," said Debbie. "I've been a Christian all my life. I've grown up in the Catholic Church. I was baptized as a baby and confirmed at age ten and never missed contrafraternity until . . . until I quit going when I was in high school."

Her callers waited patiently until she was finished, and then said, "That really isn't what we mean. We were wondering if you have a personal relationship with Jesus Christ." They then proceeded to tell Debbie about a time in each of their lives when they first experienced the love and forgiveness of Jesus Christ.

They carefully explained how God loved her. That he had a plan for Debbie's life. That he wanted to bring peace to her heart. They told her how sin had separated her from God and had made it impossible to experience that love and that peace.

They continued to read from a little booklet[1], and Debbie carefully followed each word. She looked closely as simple dia-

---

1. *Steps to Peace with God*, Billy Graham Evangelistic Association, Box 779, Minneapolis, MN 55440.

grams were employed to illustrate the distance that sin had created between God and man.

She saw that good works and religion and philosophy and morality could not bridge the distance between God and man— and then saw that the only remedy was Jesus Christ.

This was not a new message to Debbie. She had heard about Jesus Christ since she was a small child . . . but she couldn't remember having heard anything about a personal relationship before.

When she was asked to evaluate her present condition, she studied the words carefully. There were two lists. One list represented man without God and was described by such words as:

Sin
Separation
Frustration
Guilt
Lack of purpose

The other list represented man with God and was described as:

Forgiveness
Peace
Abundant life
Eternal life

The young woman reading the booklet looked straight at Debbie and asked, "Which list represents your life right now, Debbie?"

There was no hesitation, only perplexity. Debbie wondered how these strangers knew so much about her as she pointed to the words that described man without God.

Jesus Christ was then pictured as being outside the door of her heart and knocking to gain entrance.

"Is there any reason why you cannot receive Jesus Christ right now?" she was asked.

"No," she said. Her eyes filled with tears at the sight of such words as *forgiveness, peace, abundant life,* and *eternal life.*

She looked at the faces of her new friends.

"What do I have to do?"

Her attention was drawn again to the little booklet. It listed four things.

1. Admit your need. (I am a sinner.)

Debbie had no problem with this one.

2. Be willing to turn from your sins (repent).

Nor this one. There was nothing in her past that she wanted back again . . . except Jennifer.

3. Believe that Jesus Christ died on the cross for your sins and rose from the grave.

She had always believed this.

4. Through prayer, invite Jesus Christ to come in and control your life (receive him as Lord and Savior).

Debbie hadn't prayed for years, and even then she couldn't remember talking to God in her own words.

"I don't know how to pray," she said.

"You don't have to. There's a little prayer written on the next page. You can pray it to God or you can pray in your own words. All you need to do is talk to God and tell him you're sorry for your sins and ask him to forgive you."

Debbie bowed her head and began to read the words aloud: *"Dear Lord Jesus, I know that I'm a sinner and need your forgiveness. I believe that you died for my sins. I want to turn from my sins. I now invite you to come into my heart and life. I want to trust you as Savior and follow you as Lord, in the fellowship of your church."*

"Did you pray this prayer?" Debbie was asked when she finished.

"Yes," she replied.

"Did you sincerely ask Jesus Christ to come into your life?"

"Yes."

"Where is he right now?"

"I'm not sure I understand what you mean."

"If Jesus promised to come into your life if you invited him to do so . . . and if you just invited him to do that, then where is Jesus right now?"

Debbie thought for a moment and then asked, "In my life?"

"Certainly, in your life. And he has brought his peace and his forgiveness and his life with him. Jesus Christ is in your life and he has brought everything he has to offer you right along with him."

Debbie cried quietly . . . peacefully . . . thankfully. Something had just happened that she couldn't explain. Something was gone from her life—and this time it was not something she had wanted to keep, it was something she had desperately wanted to lose. She felt light, but not empty. Free but not alone. She felt forgiven for the first time in her life.

Debbie slept soundly that night . . . the sleep of peace.

CHAPTER ELEVEN

The wedding was simple but beautiful. Both Steve's and Debbie's parents were present. It was small—but still the church wedding Debbie had dreamed of, except that it was a pastor instead of a priest officiating.

As soon as possible, the happy couple climbed into their red Camaro and headed north.

They drove leisurely to Olympia and then headed west through Shelton, the Christmas Tree Capital of the World, and wound for more than an hour along the scenic shores of Hood Canal.

It was early evening when they passed Discovery Bay and stopped at the crest of a hill overlooking Port Townsend, one of Washington State's most historic and fascinating cities: a century-old community almost completely surrounded by expansive bodies of water, with snow-capped peaks forming a backdrop in every direction.

Steve drove along the waterfront, past the fleets of fishing vessels, the numerous antique shops, and quaint old brick buildings, and then turned up the hill to the upper town where they admired the largest collection of Victorian architecture north of San Francisco.

Reservations had been made at the James House, a

hundred-year-old Victorian mansion built by one of the area's wealthiest businessmen. They passed the fragrant flower gardens, climbed the steps to the porch, and sat down in the swing to take in the panorama of beauty spread out before them.

They were ushered to the Bridal Suite, a full-blown Victorian extravaganza and the most luxurious accommodation available to them in the substantial old mansion.

A single red rose greeted them. It stood in the center of a handsomely carved table near a bottle of champagne cooling in a silver bucket.

They studied the panels of walnut burl that made up the magnificent headboard, the Victorian rocker, and the long, red fainting couch. Debbie sat in an armchair placed in the four-window bay that provided a breathtaking view of the Strait of Juan de Fuca, Vancouver Island, Whidby Island, Puget Sound, Mt. Baker, and the Cascade Range to the north.

The spot was perfect for a honeymooning couple. The privacy, the beautifully romantic surroundings, the intimate decor, and their deep and compelling love for each other combined to overwhelm them.

They moved into a little world all their own. For the next few hours, they shut tight its massive door and completely forgot that anyone or anything else had ever existed. They made love with total abandon and complete satisfaction . . . Steve for the first time in his life and Debbie for the first time free of any fear or guilt or shame.

The bliss and beauty of it all, however, was shattered by the thoughtless flip of a television knob. Debbie sat transfixed as she watched a frantic mother in search of her lost daughter. It only took a few minutes for Debbie to lose complete control. She began to sob.

Steve knew all about Tim and Mike and Ken. He knew all about the abortion clinics and he knew all about Jennifer. Debbie had secured limited visitation privileges and they had driven together to Virginia's house numerous times, but the visits were always less than satisfactory. Jennifer's grandmother would either refuse to answer the door, or would allow no privacy whatever. One of the first projects the newlyweds would undertake was an all-out legal battle to get mother and daughter reunited.

There was another project that they had discussed. Debbie

wanted another baby . . . one that was all their own . . . one they could love . . . one they could keep. A doctor had removed Debbie's IUD, and from the first night of their honeymoon, they dismissed any thought of caution or contraception.

Both projects were forgotten as Steve moved to Debbie's side in an attempt to comfort her. There was no comfort possible. Debbie began reliving what she called seven wasted years. Each memory sent her into deeper depression. Thoughts of Jennifer and feelings of shame for her neglect turned a joyful honeymoon into a season of sadness.

They stayed in the charming James House for four more days. Debbie tried to fight back the black clouds that seemed determined to settle over her spirit. She tried hard to be happy—for Steve's sake.

Steve was sensitive and tender. Debbie became more distant—more inconsolable—as the hours went by. She was losing the battle to depression. They made no attempt to make love again on their honeymoon.

Debbie cried a lot . . . even after they returned to their apartment in Everett. She developed colitis, unbearable headaches, and a strong aversion to bright lights and loud noises. She felt constant pain from her ovaries. The headaches grew worse until she was finally admitted to the University Hospital for a battery of physical examinations.

After extensive tests, it was determined that Debbie had something called pseudotumor cerebri, a malady characterized by a slight swelling of the brain due to excessive fluid; a polycystic ovary disease; and an infection of the fallopian tubes.

She asked the doctor cautiously, "Could these things be caused by an abortion?"

"That's hard to say," he answered. "Any or all of the problems you're encountering right now could be directly or indirectly caused by abortion. How many abortions have you had?"

"Three," answered Debbie.

"Are you having any other problems?" Debbie told him about the nightmares and about the feelings of revulsion she at times had toward Steve. Feelings that seemed to be uncontrollable and completely out of character.

"There are times I don't want him to even touch me," she added. "I can't understand it. I know that I love him and that he loves me. Steve is the greatest thing that has ever happened to me, but there are times I can't stand him.

"My sister brought her new baby to see me last week. I didn't want to talk to her. I didn't want to even look at her little baby. I can't understand that either, because right now Steve and I are trying to have a baby of our own. Even that seems strange. I've always been able to get pregnant . . . even when I didn't want to. Now when I really want to, I can't."

"Debbie, you may need some extensive help in order to relieve these problems. You may need psychiatric as well as medical help. Would you be willing to seek counseling if I recommended it?"

"Certainly," replied Debbie. "Steve and I have already agreed to anything that's needed. He said just the other day that what abortion has done to me is the strongest argument he knows against it.

"The thing I can't understand, though, is that now that I'm trying to do what's right, everything seems to be going wrong. I thought that once I was happily married and going to church and not messing around like I used to, everything would be fine. Right now I feel worse than ever."

"The past has a way of catching up with us, Debbie. I've a hunch that there are some things in your past that need to be faced before you're ever going to be completely well and happy. We might even need to run some tests to find out why you can't get pregnant, but we'll wait a few more months before we do that."

Debbie made an appointment for a spinal tap, took a small stack of signed prescription forms with her, and left wondering if her life would ever be what she had once dreamed . . . wondering if she had given up one baby too many . . . wondering if Jennifer would ever be hers again.

CHAPTER TWELVE

"What is the most painful thing that has ever happened to you?"

Debbie looked long and hard at the psychiatrist who sat behind the large walnut desk that separated them. She searched intently for an answer to his question and then finally said, "I can't name one. I've had nothing but painful things happen to me for as long as I can remember."

Debbie began rehearsing a story of shattered romances, broken promises, and physical and sexual abuse. She named a long list of men who had exploited her . . . even raped her. Abortionists had "torn" three unborn children from her body. One boyfriend had actually run over her with a car in an unsuccessful attempt to kill her. Her own ex-husband's mother had "stolen" her child, and the courts had refused to allow her to regain custody. One boyfriend had introduced her to marijuana, and another had started her drinking.

She listed the physical ailments that had been diagnosed and then suggested that her depression was now causing her to eat endlessly and her weight was completely out of control.

"How do you feel, Debbie, about all of these people who have hurt you?"

"I hate them!" Debbie exploded. "I hate them all! I think, if I could, I'd kill them. They have completely ruined my life. I

73

thought if I could just find a good husband, everything would be fine. I've found a good husband and I still can't sleep and I can't work and I can't think. The memories are haunting me. I can't get rid of them."

"Of all of these painful memories, Debbie, is there one that hurts more than the others?" he asked.

Debbie thought for a long time and then began to cry. "I'll never forgive my father and my mother for making me have that first abortion." She told the story of Tim and her first pregnancy and the Columbia River Medical Clinic and the deep humiliation and pain she had suffered when she was not allowed to keep her first child.

"My father wrote me a letter," she said, as she reached into her purse. The letter was well worn with constant folding and unfolding. It read:

> Dear Debbie:
> Your mother and I are anxious to hear from you. We have no idea where you are. We got your message from the runaway hot line that you were all right, but we still didn't know how to reach you.
> We've heard just enough to know that your life has been awfully hard.
> Virginia called and said she still has Jennifer and that you haven't contacted her.
> Debbie, we're awfully sorry for all the mistakes you've made. We're sorry for the mistakes we've made. Somehow we feel that if we hadn't forced you to have that first abortion, none of this would ever have happened.
> Will you forgive us?
> Your Dad

"That letter was written last year, before I met Steve," she explained. "I've seen them many times before and after the wedding. We get along all right, but none of us has ever mentioned that abortion in Hood River."

"Why haven't you talked about the abortion?"

"They refuse to bring it up."

"Have you ever thought of bringing it up?"

"No."

"How do you feel about the unborn babies you aborted?"

"Terrible."

He waited.

"Guilty . . . sad . . . angry . . . I've often wished there was some way I could tell them how sorry I am." She began to weep. "If I could only talk to them and ask them to forgive me. Everyone I've asked has said that they were really not human beings, but somehow I can't believe that. I feel little eyes staring at me and pleading with me to tell the doctors to stop. I didn't stop. I just let them do it. I let him kill my little babies."

"Would you like to talk to one of those babies, Debbie?"

"Oh, yes . . . if only I could. I can't sleep nights. I feel so condemned for what I've done."

Her counselor got up from behind his desk, walked around to Debbie, helped her up, and then placed an empty chair in the center of the room. He seated Debbie in another chair facing it, and then seated himself behind her, out of her range of vision.

"Debbie," he said, "I want you to forget that I'm in this room with you. For a little while, I'm going to be completely silent. I want you to imagine that the empty chair in front of you is your little baby . . . the baby that you had aborted in the Columbia River Medical Clinic."

"How old was it?" he asked.

"Just twelve weeks," she answered.

"How was it aborted?"

"By suction."

"How did you feel when it was happening?"

"I kept asking it to forgive me. All the time that tube was inside of me tearing that little baby out of me, I kept telling it how sorry I was . . . that I couldn't help it . . . they were making me do it . . ."

"Why don't you talk to your baby now? Just pretend that chair is your baby. Forget that I'm here and tell it what you think it wants to hear."

Debbie looked at the empty chair for a long time. It was hard to visualize anything but a chair in front of her. But the longer she looked, the longer she thought, the more she sensed something happening down deep inside of her. She felt pain . . . she felt sorrow . . . she felt anguish . . . she felt an emptiness that gripped and tore at her until her whole body began to convulse with sobs.

She slid down to the floor and knelt in front of an empty chair and buried her head in its cushion.

"Oh, my baby, my baby," she cried. "I'm so sorry. Please forgive me. I didn't mean to do it. I didn't want to do it. I wouldn't have hurt you for anything in the world.

"All I wanted to do was to hold you and to nurse you and to change you and to feed you.

"I wanted to love you. Tim wanted to love you. We both wanted to love you together. You were our baby. You were the result of our love and we wanted to keep you, but they wouldn't let us.

"I miss you so much. At nights I can hear you crying for me. I get up to get a bottle and I find it's only a dream.

"I wanted to feel your little head on my arm, on my breast, against my cheek. I wanted to buy you little clothes and wrap you in little blankets. I wanted to look at you while you were sleeping and watch you when you were awake.

"I wanted to help you take your first step and listen to you speak your first word. I wanted to buy your first shoes and fix your meals.

"I wanted to watch you leave for your first day at school and then have you come home and tell me all about it. I wanted you . . . I want you. I still want you . . ."

Suddenly Debbie groaned and wailed as if the intense pain was more than she could bear.

"I'm sorry," she screamed. "I'm sorry, please, please forgive me."

She slid from the chair in an exhausted heap . . . completely spent—emptied of one emotion that she'd been suppressing for years.

A wise and compassionate counselor reached down and lifted Debbie to her feet and wrapped his arms around her and held her tight until the sobs finally stopped.

CHAPTER THIRTEEN

Every attempt to regain custody of Jennifer met with failure.
Steve and Debbie wrote Henry and Virginia Williams asking
for more liberal visitation rights. The only visits Virginia would
allow took place in a suburban shopping mall in which Debbie
and Jennifer were never allowed any privacy.

Virginia's attorney responded to their request by stating,

In reviewing the facts, it appears to me that visitation will continue as it has in the past until you can
show the Williamses that you have become mature
enough to handle visitation outside the scope of someone else's supervision.

It appears that you have had some problems and the
Williamses deeply and honestly feel that the best thing
for Jennifer is to remain in their custody until she is old
enough to make a decision or at such time as a guar-
dian *ad litem* would state that it is in the best interests
of Jennifer to reside with you.

The overriding purpose of the Williams's involve-
ment during this entire last four years has been Jennifer's best interests. Unfortunately, it appears that you
have selfishly considered your interests above hers. To

now want and ask for her return seems very good for you, but not in the best interest of Jennifer.

If you have any further thoughts or comments, please put them in writing to the Williamses or to myself.

The Williams's attorney filed a motion with the court to sever all of Jennifer's parental rights. The judge refused to honor the motion.

Steve and Debbie secured an attorney, borrowed $2,000 for a retainer plus another $600 for a case worker's report, and proceeded to work to gain full custody of Jennifer.

Their attorney's first reaction was positive and encouraging. He stated:

> I have completed my review of your comments and all of the legal papers you forwarded to me. There was a lot of material to absorb but I believe that you should have a reasonable chance to be successful in court if you should begin action to reclaim the custody of your daughter.
>
> Your original temporary custody order permits you to petition for custody of your child. The standard of proof for you to obtain custody would be those in any dissolution action and would depend upon the best interest of the child.
>
> It bothers me now that you have not confronted your mother-in-law sooner.
>
> You will need to secure proof that your marriage is stable, that you are financially able to care for your child, and that your home would be a good environment for a growing child.

Steve and Debbie began securing letters that could be presented in court to prove their worth as prospective parents.

Debbie had provided child care in her home to supplement their income. One mother wrote:

> I never felt any hesitation in leaving my six-year-old son and nine-month-old baby with Debbie. She was always patient and loving to both of them. In fact, my son used to beg to go to her house.

Debbie is better than average with children. I really feel that Debbie deserves custody of Jennifer.

Debbie's sister wrote:

Steve and Debbie are mature adults and will do a great job raising Jennifer. Debbie deserves to get her little girl back.

An endocrinologist who had treated Debbie stated:

Debbie's physical fitness at this time appears to be sound and her depression hopefully will respond to the restoration of the child to her home.

A friend wrote,

Steve and Debbie's marriage was made in heaven. They have many things in common such as an appreciation of fine art, love of music, and love of people.

Debbie has suffered much anxiety and punished herself unduly because she hasn't taken proper care of her little girl.

Even Debbie's parents included a letter to the court. It read:

Steve and Debbie have been married nearly two years and have established a close, loving relationship with each other.

They have experienced the usual economic difficulties of a newly married couple, but these problems are now behind them and they are mature enough and economically strong enough to care for a child.

Another sister wrote,

Debbie has matured considerably since she moved away from home. She seems to be taking her responsibilities seriously. In my opinion, Steve and Debbie love Jennifer very much. I feel that she should be with them.

Many testified in letters that Debbie had become a Christian and an active member of a church and that she appeared to be able to provide a Christian environment for her child.

Their counselor, a clinical member of the American Association of Marriage and Family Therapy, stated that he saw them now as a loving couple, capable of raising Jennifer and any other children they might have.

Another counseling service listed eight reasons in strong support of custody.

1. Debbie has come to terms with her physical and mental health and has developed positive attitudes toward living.
2. Steve and Debbie have built a strong marriage.
3. Steve continues to be employed with the Boeing Company in a job which has a future.
4. Jennifer misses the companionship of her real mother.
5. Both Steve and Debbie are church members and believe in the religious training of children.
6. Neither Steve nor Debbie are abusive users of alcohol.
7. Both Steve and Debbie show concern for the child and have already set up guidelines for its training.
8. Now is the time for Steve and Debbie to have the daughter. They desire her return and are ready to parent her.

The case worker employed by the attorney spent weeks securing information from anyone at all knowledgeable about the situation. She investigated Steve and Debbie and Henry and Virginia. Her extensive report encouraged the court to give custody to Steve and Debbie.

Their attorney wrote:

Things are progressing nicely on this end. The evaluation of your case worker will be invaluable to us.

The next step is to prepare the necessary papers for a court hearing.

The court hearing was held in the Superior Court of the State of Washington in the City of Seattle on the seventeenth day of December, just eight years to the very day that Debbie learned of her first pregnancy.

The judge ruled against giving custody of Jennifer to Steve and Debbie.

It was a difficult decision. The court was forced to determine which home could provide a better environment for a five-year-old. It was forced to acknowledge that Debbie was not qualified to mother her own child while at the same time acknowledging that she had made significant progress in rehabilitating her life.

The judge found no support for the charges of child abuse but couldn't ignore the reality of child neglect.

Debbie was forced to publicly name every man with whom she had ever engaged in sexual relations and to state the number of times they had engaged in sex.

Her abortions were made public. The question was asked:

How can this court decide in favor of giving a child over to the custody of a woman who has aborted three children?

The opposing attorney further stated,

It's obvious that this woman is depressed and living on anti-depressants, and is fat and has had multiple abortions. Who would want a fat slob like this for a mother?

Debbie screamed at the speaker when she heard those words, and in her total frustration proceeded to bang her head against the table.

The presiding judge stated clearly that,

Jennifer is in the Williams family solely as the result of the conduct of Debbie.

Visitation rights were granted. Jennifer was permitted to spend Christmas Eve with her mother, and a review was ordered for one year.

Steve and Debbie were devastated. They had been so certain of victory. Their church friends had prayed . . .

Debbie confronted her attorney in the hallway. Her anger was intense.

"You told me to get an abortion or I wouldn't be able to get my child back. They told me I couldn't have my child back because I'd gotten an abortion. Thanks a lot."

A consoling letter was written by the appointed case worker that read,

> I do believe that you folks should have gained custody of your child. I reported that you were fit. I am sorry for the way you were humiliated.
>
> The court cannot take away from you the progress you have made, nor your belief in God, nor Steve's love for you.
>
> Do your grieving and then get back to the business of living and pray that someday Jennifer will be yours.
>
> I am truly sorry and my heart and prayers go out for you.

In her deep sadness, Debbie wrote down her thoughts of Jennifer:

> I close my eyes, I see you there
> in your bed, I touch your hair
> I kiss your cheek, I wonder if
> you know how much I care.
>
> Child of mine, I love you so
> you are my dream and where
> you are, I cannot go.
>
> They say that you can't live with me
> It is not best for you
> How could they say that? Is it true?
>
> Child of mine, I bore you in much pain
> but like Jesus said, I forgot about the pain
> because of the joy I had in my heart at
> loving you.
>
> You were put on my tummy
> soft and purple
> the cord that united us pulsated
> then was cut
> but it did not cut away my love
> bone of my bone, flesh of my flesh.

I believe in resurrections
and the bright morning star
I believe that Jesus knows where you are
and that his angels guard you
and will guide you back to me.

CHAPTER FOURTEEN

"It seems like everyone else can have a baby . . . but every four weeks I'm reminded that Steve and I have failed again."

"I think I can help you, Debbie," Dr. Lawson replied. "With recently developed drugs, modern diagnostic techniques, and new surgical procedures, we are finding that in nine out of ten cases of infertility, we are able to identify the problem, and in about seventy percent of those we can help couples have children within a reasonable period of time."

"Doctor, do you think that my abortions have made it impossible for me to have a baby? In every one of the release forms I signed, there was the mention of sterility as a possible consequence. The counselors told me that statement was just routine protection for the doctor and that they knew of no one who had ever become sterile."

"You've asked me that question before, Debbie, and I really don't have any more of an informed answer now than I did then. I will tell you this, though: You have obviously been fertile. You have a daughter and you have terminated three pregnancies by abortion. In the days when abortions were performed illegally, it was not uncommon to find damage done to the reproductive organs through the use of instruments which were not properly sterilized. That still happens, but not as often. Even legal

abortions performed in approved facilities under competent sur-
veillance are sometimes followed by infection or damage to the
fallopian tubes. These complications are treatable and are usually
resolved quickly with proper care.

"But the only way we can be sure, Debbie, is to organize a
basic study of both you and your husband that will first require
that you fill out a confidential fertility questionnaire. This form
will give me information that I don't presently have available.

"It's very important that you answer every question fully
and honestly. Some of the questions are very personal in nature.
If you have difficulty answering these, please consult with me.

"I'll want a complete medical and surgical history. It's important that you tell me about every surgical experience you've had.

"I'll also want a complete sexual history. This may be
difficult, Debbie. I know you have tried to forget your past. Stir-
ring up all of these memories may be painful, but it is very important.

"Your psychosomatic history is also vital. You've told me
about your bouts with depression over your inability to secure
Jennifer. Stress can cause you not to be able to conceive.

"I'll do a thorough physical examination. Your weight problem may tell me something; even your struggle with acne has
some bearing on infertility.

"I'll examine your genital tract for infection, polyps, cervical
tears. I'll measure the size of your uterus and determine its position. I'll look for the presence of possible tumors.

"Our lab will need a urine specimen, and they'll do a complete blood work up. We'll even have to test you for the possibility
of syphilis. I'll probably order a basic endocrine study in your
case.

"Steve's fertility will need to be established. We'll need his
complete medical and surgical history. We'll also need an occupa-
tional history. It may be that your husband has been exposed to
chemicals or x-rays or radar that could have affected him.

"We'll do a thorough physical examination of your husband
and collect laboratory data as well.

"I'll counsel with you both about methods and techniques
of having intercourse. The solution to your problem may be as
simple as changing physical positions.

"If nothing is discovered up to this point that could be causing your inability to become pregnant, we may find it necessary to move on to more sophisticated tests. We may want to pass some carbon dioxide gas through your fallopian tubes to be certain that they are both open and not obstructed by adhesions or a filmy scar tissue.

"We may even insert an instrument directly into the pelvis in order to see all the pelvic organs . . . the uterus, the ovaries, and the tubes . . . and even test the tubes visually. Of course this is done under fairly heavy sedation so you won't feel any pain or discomfort.

"Laparoscopy is another technique we use," he continued. "A viewing instrument is inserted through a small incision in the abdomen, and we pump a little gas in to push the other organs aside. With this procedure we can get our best view of the tubes and other possible problem areas. We usually do this last, Debbie, because it requires general anesthesia—it's technically a surgical procedure.

"It's been more than four years that you and Steve have been trying to have your baby, and I think that tells us we should probably go ahead with the entire testing program.

"It may take as long as three months and may cost as much as a thousand dollars."

Steve and Debbie pursued the entire infertility study diligently and with high hopes. Steve's sperm count was a little low, but not enough to pose a problem. Some adhesions were found in Debbie that were restricting the function of the fallopian tubes. Tubal surgery was indicated.

Steve and Debbie were advised about the surgery and told that tubal surgery was actually a reconstructive process. "We don't remove anything," Dr. Lawson explained. "Our goal is to completely preserve the function of the tube while removing anything that may hamper it in its reproductive process.

"The tests indicate that this could be a sufficient problem to prevent pregnancy. Tuboplasty—that's what we call the surgical process—isn't always successful, though. It's sort of a last-resort procedure, and the success rate is not very encouraging. Only about fifty percent of our surgical patients are completely corrected by this procedure."

"Could this problem be caused by my abortion, Doctor?" Debbie asked.

"Again, Debbie, it's impossible for me to answer your question with any degree of certainty," he replied. "The fact that you had some pelvic infection after your third abortion might suggest that possibility. But there's no way to be absolutely certain."

"When can I have the surgery?"

"Just as soon as we can set up a schedule for you. You both realize the risks. It's certainly not life-threatening, but I can't guarantee that it will solve your problem."

Six months after what appeared to be a successful surgery, Debbie was still unable to get pregnant.

CHAPTER FIFTEEN

"Any woman who has an abortion is an animal!"[1]

This statement from the lips of a television preacher startled both Steve and Debbie. They listened intently as the internationally known evangelist spoke of the nearly one and a half million babies that are murdered annually by abortion. The evangelist described it as "America's Greatest Crime."

Debbie sent for a copy of his message and asked also for his monthly publication. She was not prepared for what she read or what she saw.

Page four of one of the periodicals contained an actual-size photograph of a fourteen-week-old fetus resting upright within a balloon-shaped placenta. It was fully formed. Its left ear was clearly visible. She could see one closed eye, a little nose, and a fully-formed mouth. It was holding hands with itself. The distinct little fingers and thumb of the right hand were relaxed and almost folded over the left thumb. Even the fingernails appeared to be visible.

Debbie carefully studied the little shoulder, the upper arm, elbow, the forearm, and wrist—all appearing to be fully developed.

---

1. Jimmy Swaggart, "America's Greatest Crime," *The Evangelist*, November 1983, p. 5.

The umbilical cord looked like a piece of corded rope that wrapped itself loosely around the back of the head, over the shoulder, and then attached itself to the child's stomach.

The rib cage was prominent. Ribs could be seen through what appeared to be almost glasslike skin. The veins could be traced over the whole body with relative ease.

The legs seemed relaxed, with one fully developed foot resting upon another. The baby appeared to be at peace . . . and it was obviously a baby. As Debbie studied it, her suspicions were confirmed.

This was not just an accumulation of cells or a mass of protoplasm. This was not just an impersonal "blob" as some had told her. She even resisted calling this a fetus. This was a baby, and this baby was almost the same age as two of the babies she had aborted.

Debbie read the entire article carefully. She resisted the term *murder* as it was used repeatedly. It was difficult to accept the statement which read:

> To God, any unprovoked killing is murder, and the person guilty of murder is deserving of punishment. To him there is no difference between the person who kills an unborn child and the person who pulls the trigger of a gun in a robbery.[2]

The grisly pictures that followed were too much for Debbie—actual case studies with accompanying photographs that displayed the remains of babies aborted by "D & C's" and suction and by salt poisoning. The dismembered remains of a twelve-week-old fetus caused her to stop. Her tears began to cause little spots to form on the page. The pictures became blurred as Debbie began to weep.

"How can people do this?" she cried. "How could I have done this? Am I really an animal for having those abortions?"

These were questions she asked of her pastor the next day. Debbie had spent a sleepless night—talking, praying, tossing. She needed answers.

"Debbie, I'm awfully sorry for all the pain you've suffered over the last ten years. I wish there were some way we could turn

---

2. Ibid., p. 7.

back the pages of the calendar and start over again. I wish there were a way to completely erase the memories that continue to haunt you. I feel so helpless at times. There are so many things that I would like to be able to do but cannot.

"For every choice there is a consequence. Some are good; some are bad. Some are temporary. Some are permanent. That seems to be one of the changeless laws of life. It's a law that sometimes haunts all of us.

"Yes, Debbie, I believe that abortion on demand is the needless killing of unborn babies—and I believe that this practice is extracting a terribly heavy payment from many who have it done to them.

"It has cost you more than you can afford to pay. You have suffered mentally and physically. You have lost your daughter and suffered humiliation and stress. For this, I'm terribly sorry.

"For all of this you have been forgiven. When you established a personal relationship with Jesus Christ, he forgave you. He forgave you for each of those abortions. He forgave you for your neglect of Jennifer. He forgave you for everything you have ever done that was displeasing to him or injurious to yourself.

"In forgiveness, God also forgets. He forgets everything— that's his promise. The trouble is that we cannot. Our memories are too vivid . . . too deeply etched in our minds. We'd like to erase them, but we cannot. Those memories oftentimes stay with us until we die.

"Tell me, Debbie, have you ever forgiven your parents for requiring you to have that first abortion?"

"I'll never forgive them for that," she replied. "My dad told me that he thought that was the beginning of all my problems, and I agree, but I'll never forgive them. They're responsible for every problem I've ever had."

"That's not true, Debbie. They are not responsible for every problem that you have ever had. They have contributed to some of your problems. Planned Parenthood has possibly contributed to some of your problems. Your boyfriends have contributed to some of your problems. The secular society you live in has contributed to some of your problems. Circumstances have contributed to some of your problems.

"Debbie, you have become a changed woman in these past few years. I don't know when I've seen such a dramatic change in a person. Your ministry to troubled women has been remarkably effective. The nursery department couldn't survive without you. You're one of the hardest-working people I have ever known. You attack each new job with a frenzy, and you always complete it successfully. You're a real tribute to God's grace, Debbie, and I'm so proud to be your pastor.

"But I'm going to level with you. I'm going to be as direct and as blunt as I know how—and when I do this, I realize that I may lose a very good friend. But I must tell you what I think is the truth.

"You will never be at peace with yourself and with God and with your parents—even with your husband—until you finally accept full and complete responsibility for all that's happened.

"Do you understand what I'm saying? Your problems did not begin with your abortion. They began in your mind when you first started developing your relationship with Tim Beezley. When you refused to say no to Tim in the back seat of that car, for whatever reason, that was when your problems finally passed beyond your ability to control them. It wasn't the abortion, Debbie. Without that pregnancy, there would have been no need for an abortion.

"I'm old-fashioned enough, Debbie, to believe that our present moral standard is really immoral—even though the whole world seems to have adopted it. I believe that God has designed that the ideal relationship is to be found between one man and one woman for a lifetime. Abortion is not our problem. It's only a symptom of a greater problem . . . the problem of sexual irresponsibility. Abortion is the consequence of a long string of poor choices. It only solves the problem of pregnancy. The problems it creates are far greater.

"Have you ever asked God's forgiveness for that one thoughtless, seemingly unimportant act that started all of your problems?"

Debbie was quiet for a long moment before she spoke. "No," she said, "I've never even thought about it. Do you think I should?"

"Certainly, I think you should. But what I think really isn't all that important, Debbie. It's what *God* thinks that really matters—and this is something God tells us to do if we want to experience complete forgiveness."

Debbie had been conditioned to ask forgiveness ever since that night the two young women called in her home. It was not hard, but asking forgiveness so specifically was different . . . and asking forgiveness for something she had thought was someone else's fault was different.

"Please forgive me, Father, for what Tim and I did. And— please forgive me for the way I've blamed everyone else and for the way I've hated my parents, and please, Father, give me the courage to ask their forgiveness for all the pain I've caused them.

"Thank you, Father, for helping me to see today what I have never been able to see before. Amen."

*   *   *

Debbie continues to minister effectively to unwed mothers and small children.

Debbie continues to hope for the return of her daughter.

Debbie continues to pray for another baby of her own.

And Debbie continues to remember . . . as hard as she tries to forget . . . she continues to remember.

Author's Note

It is estimated that nearly fifteen million unborn babies have died from legal abortions in the United States since they were legalized by the Supreme Court in 1973.

For every unborn child that dies, there is a mother who suffers varying degrees of physical, emotional, or spiritual pain. Some have died. Some, like Debbie, are slowly and painfully unraveling the tangled webs of a life that has become terribly complicated because of an unwise choice.

There are alternatives to abortion and there are agencies available and prepared to give counsel to women who find themselves in need of help.

Crisis pregnancy centers are now located in more than 120 cities in the United States and Canada. These centers are developed and coordinated by the Christian Action Council, an organization that was founded in 1975 in the home of Dr. Billy Graham.

The Pearson Foundation, a Catholic agency, has 200 centers in the United States and Canada and is planning to establish centers in India and Peru.

Thomas Road Baptist Church in Lynchburg, Virginia, has facilities and care available. They also make referrals across the country.

These centers or agencies usually offer:

- Free pregnancy testing
- Education on abortion and alternatives
- Housing
- Prenatal, childbirth, and breastfeeding information

- Clothing
- Classes for the single parent
- Referrals for medical care, free legal assistance, or other community services
- Ongoing counseling and friendship

All of these services are usually free and always confidential. Locations and phone numbers can be secured from:

The Christian Action Council
422 C Street N. E.
Washington, D. C. 20002
(1-202-544-1720)

The Pearson Foundation
3663 Lindell Blvd.
Suite 290
St. Louis, MO 63108
(1-800-633-2252, ext. 700)

Thomas Road Baptist Church
Lynchburg, Virginia 24501
(1-800-368-3336)